PLAYS OF THE AMERICAN EXPERIENCE

25 Fascinating Scenes
for the Classroom or Stage

THOMAS HISCHAK

MERIWETHER PUBLISHING
A division of Pioneer Drama Service, Inc.
Denver, Colorado

Meriwether Publishing
A division of Pioneer Drama Service, Inc.
PO Box 4267
Englewood, CO 80155-4267

www.pioneerdrama.com

Editors: Kristin Ettinger and Rebecca Johnson
Cover design: Devin Watson
Project manager: Lori Conary
Text design: Lori Conary

Printed in the United States of America
First Edition

Library of Congress Cataloging-in-Publication Data

Names: Hischak, Thomas S., author.
Title: Plays of the American Experience : 25 fascinating scenes for the
    classroom or stage / by Thomas Hischak.
Description: First edition. | Englewood, CO : Meriwether Publishing, a
    division of Pioneer Drama Service, Inc., [2018]
Identifiers: LCCN 2018003228 | ISBN 9781566082259 (pbk. : alk. paper)
Subjects: LCSH: United States–Social life and customs–Drama. | United
    States–History–Drama. | Young adult drama, American. | LCGFT: Drama.
Classification: LCC PS3558.I76 P53 2018 | DDC 812/.54–dc23
LC record available at https://lccn.loc.gov/2018003228

1   2   3   18   19   20

CONTENTS

ACKNOWLEDGEMENTS

I wish to thank the people who helped me in the development of these plays by participating in readings and making corrections and suggestions. Among them are Bob and Jackie Sanders, Andrea McCook, Heather Cribbs, and Erik Bodien. A special thanks to Karen Bullock and Lori Conary at Pioneer Drama Service. Finally, my continuing gratitude and appreciation for Cathy Hischak, who helps and encourages me in all my writing projects.

FOREWORD

When Thomas Hischak approached me about doing a reading of *Plays of the American Experience* in my advanced theatre classes, I knew it would be a learning experience for everyone involved. I never could have imagined, however, that my students would latch on to the material like they did. Each story was so engaging that they immediately wanted to dive into performances of the material, rather than just reading it. A handful of my students asked if they could use the scenes in class as duet or ensemble scenes. Others wanted them for their Theatre 3 directing assignment. One of my students even requested to use a condensed version of the book for his Senior Conservatory!

These scenes are well-suited for middle school as well as high school. I can see myself doing an in-class production with my Theatre 1 classes. Each vignette is short enough that developing actors won't feel overwhelmed at the prospect of memorizing lines, yet rich enough that they're able to build a genuine character and tell a real story. These would also work well for teaching about the structure of a play—the conflict and resolution for each character and the scene as a whole, how characters feel about each other and their situation, the subtext of what a character is thinking but not saying.

As beneficial as this collection of ten-minute plays is for a drama class, it can also be wonderfully valuable in classrooms beyond the walls of the theatre department. A student or teacher does not need to have a drama background to utilize and enjoy reading these plays. These bite-sized pieces of history are very easy to digest and understand. They're short enough to keep students interested, yet long enough to teach a powerful lesson. And the Background and Aftermath sections that bookend each scene add depth and meaning to each moment in history.

So who else might enrich their curriculum with this book? Theatrical literature is a staple in English classes, and Hischak's ability to bring situations and characters to life in such brief pieces speaks highly to the quality of his writing. With this book, a science teacher can bring to life the process behind an invention such as the television. Instead of reading a ten-page article on the bombing of Pearl Harbor, a history teacher can allow students to more personally experience how it affected military families in Hawaii. Rather than lecture on the effects of World War II on daily life in America, an economics class can relive what it was like to ration something we take for granted—sugar—in order to make a birthday cake. The table of contents is arranged chronologically, and the appendix at the back of the book cross-indexes these scenes by topic, making it easy to pinpoint the perfect skit to augment a lesson, no matter the era or the subject area.

As educators, we strive to find material that pertains directly to our subject yet also allows us to make connections among a multitude of subjects. *Plays of the American Experience* does just that! Besides being ideal short plays for developing acting skills, they enrich students with a deeper understanding of moments in American history, including scientific discoveries and inventions, cultural events, and accomplishments of famous people. These behind-the-scenes glimpses at life help young people develop a meaningful empathy for American citizens of the past. At its bare minimum, a reading requires no more than the script—no costumes, no sets, no stage—to bring these plays to life. On the flip side, one or more can be performed in fully-staged splendor for classroom, festival, or contest use. Without a doubt, this compendium of short plays is a sound investment for every classroom.

Heather Cribbs, Theatre Director
Thespian Troupe 1903
New Smyrna Beach High School
New Smyrna Beach, FL

PREFACE

Imagine a time when people only learned about the past by reading history textbooks, diaries, memoirs, and historical novels. Then photography was invented and history became pictures. Movies and television made history even more visual and accessible. Finally, the internet gave us an immersive portal into the past. But there is one format for bringing history alive that dates back to early civilizations: theatre. Playgoers in Athens in the fifth century BC, for example, learned about the Trojan War and other events hundreds of years in their past through theatre. After all, what can bring the past alive better than stories performed by live actors?

The plays collected here are short theatrical pieces that aim to bring to life moments in American history from the early nineteenth century to the 1970s. Most of the characters in these plays are not famous figures nor even factual people. They are ordinary Americans who were affected by major events over which they had no control. In most cases, these characters did not make history, but they certainly lived it. Some of the plays are tragic. Others are much lighter in tone, for history is not just a series of wars and disasters. It is about people living through times of change and how they deal with those changes.

These twenty-five plays are intended for various uses in an educational setting. The plays can simply be read aloud in the classroom, with individual students assigned to certain roles regardless of the age, race, or sex of the characters. They can also be staged in the classroom with a few chairs and desks to suggest the location of the play. For the more ambitious, an actual production of a play could be staged with costumes, props, and suggested scenic pieces. Such a production could be performed at a school assembly, a public presentation, or for contest at a drama festival. Regardless of the format in which the plays are used, the purpose remains the same: to use theatre to bring American history alive.

Let me give you some practical notes. Each play runs between eight and ten minutes. The setting and costumes for each play are described fully. This is not to suggest an elaborate production, but rather to allow the teacher and the students to more fully picture the location and period where the action takes place. Each play includes a background description of the historical situation of the plot and ends with an aftermath description that explains what happened after the dramatized event. Students and teachers, however, are encouraged to do their own research about the details in each play. Who was "Uncle Miltie"? What was a "Hooverville"? Who was Charlie McCarthy? What is an icebox? What does "Loose Lips Sinks Ships" mean? Exploring these past icons will be an education in itself and greatly aid in bringing the dramatized events to life.

Thomas Hischak

WITHOUT ICE

(1845)

BACKGROUND

John Gorrie was born in the West Indies and grew up in South Carolina. He was intrigued by sicknesses that seem to prevail in hot climates. After graduating from medical school, Gorrie moved to the Gulf city of Apalachicola, Florida, where he tended patients in the US Marine Hospital. There, he treated soldiers suffering from malaria, which they contracted while serving in South America.

SETTING

TIME: July 1845.

PLACE: The laboratory inside the US Marine Hospital in Apalachicola, Florida.

CHARACTERS

DR. JOHN GORRIE (M) .... doctor specializing in malaria victims

LEONARD PORTER (M) .... patient in his twenties

NURSE WARREN (F) .... his nurse

NURSE DUNN (F) .... another

MR. PORTER (M) .... Leonard's father

MRS. PORTER (F) .... Leonard's mother

SET DESCRIPTION

There is a desk UP RIGHT with a chair behind it. A cabinet with a thermometer for taking people's temperatures stands against the UP RIGHT wall DOWNSTAGE of the desk. A table with scientific instruments is DOWN LEFT. A chair sets next to the table. A huge boxed-in machine with cabinet doors that open so the staff can operate it takes up much of the UPSTAGE wall. UP LEFT is a door with a small window in it that leads to the cooling chamber. Another door DOWN RIGHT leads to the outside hall.

PROPERTIES

Chart, wheelchair (DUNN); small watch on chain (WARREN); key (GORRIE).

SOUND EFFECTS

Loud machine running, machine turning off.

SOUND EFFECT: LOUD MACHINE RUNNING. LIGHTS UP on NURSE DUNN sitting in the chair near the table looking at her chart. She wears a period nurse's uniform. After a few moments, DR. GORRIE ENTERS RIGHT from the hall with NURSE WARREN, an older nurse wearing the same uniform. She wears a small watch on a chain pinned to her blouse. GORRIE wears a three-piece period suit and a white lab coat. DUNN rises when they come in, and there is a conversation among the three of them that we cannot hear. DUNN gives GORRIE the chart. He looks it over, then gives it to WARREN. He signals DUNN to go to the cooling room door UP LEFT. She opens it and EXITS LEFT. GORRIE crosses to the huge boxed-in machine. He unlocks the cabinet doors with a key, then pulls some levers inside and turns some unseen dials. SOUND EFFECT: MACHINE TURNING OFF. DUNN ENTERS LEFT, pushing a wheelchair with LEONARD PORTER sitting in it. He is pale, sickly, and sweating profusely in a feverish state. He wears a hospital gown.

GORRIE: Well, Leonard, how are you feeling now?

LEONARD: Still a little dizzy, Dr. Gorrie. And still sweating.

GORRIE: I see. Nurse Warren, you better take his temperature again.

WARREN: *(Efficient.)* Yes, Doctor. *(Goes to the cabinet to get a thermometer.)*

LEONARD: But it sure felt nice and cool in there. Can't I go back in for a little longer?

GORRIE: Not with the way you are perspiring. We don't want you to catch pneumonia.

WARREN: *(To LEONARD as she shakes the thermometer.)* Open, please. *(LEONARD opens his mouth, and she puts the thermometer in.)* Now close tight. *(Stares at her watch.)*

GORRIE: The purpose of the cooling room, Leonard, is to change your immediate environment. If we can create an atmosphere quite different from the one you experienced in South America, we hope to keep the malaria from thriving. Do you understand? *(LEONARD nods his head yes.)*

WARREN: *(To LEONARD, brusque.)* Keep still, please!

GORRIE: Of course, this is all just a theory of mine. A theory that has to be tested. Do you mind being a guinea pig, Leonard? *(LEONARD shakes his head no.)*

WARREN: *(Harsh.)* Please!

GORRIE: How much longer, Nurse Warren?

WARREN: *(Eyes her watch.)* Twenty-six more seconds. If the patient can remain still.

GORRIE: My fault. I'll ask you no more questions, Leonard. *(To DUNN.)* Nurse Dunn, Leonard seems to be weakening. When we are finished here, you better get him back to his bed.

DUNN: Yes, Doctor.

WARREN: Time's up! *(Takes the thermometer from LEONARD'S mouth and hands it to GORRIE, who looks at it carefully.)*

LEONARD: Is it bad, Doctor?

GORRIE: Still higher than I'd like.

WARREN: You heard the doctor, Nurse Dunn. Take the patient back to the ward.

LEONARD: I sure would like to get outside a little. I haven't been out since—

WARREN: *(To LEONARD.)* You heard the doctor's orders. *(To DUNN.)* Nurse Dunn!

DUNN: Yes, ma'am. *(Starts to wheel LEONARD RIGHT.)*

GORRIE: Nurse Dunn, why don't you take the long way back, going through the garden?

LEONARD: Thank you, Doctor.

GORRIE: A little fresh air might be good.

WARREN: It's ninety-six degrees outside!

GORRIE: It will be a little cooler in the garden. Good afternoon, Leonard. I'll see you tomorrow.

LEONARD: Certainly, Doctor. *(To DUNN.)* Nurse Dunn, the garden! (DUNN wheels LEONARD OFF RIGHT through the door. A slight pause.)*

WARREN: How high, Doctor?

GORRIE: One hundred and five.

WARREN: I see.

GORRIE: Has the patient shown any other symptoms of the malaria?

WARREN: He complains of headaches. And some days he can't keep his food down.

GORRIE: *(Discouraged.)* This time I thought I might see an improvement. The cooling room is not having the effect I had hoped for.

WARREN: It makes the young men more comfortable. All the malaria patients say so.

GORRIE: Comfortable. But the malaria rages on. I'm afraid my theory is nothing but... nonsense.

WARREN: Don't feel that way, Doctor. I think your ideas are right. You just haven't found the correct—

GORRIE: *(Bitter.)* I'm afraid I've found nothing! *(Crosses to the machine box.)* This contraption of mine is nothing more than... noise.

WARREN: Perhaps if we could get more ice.

GORRIE: In Florida? In July? What's the use? Malaria would rage in patients even if you brought them to the Arctic Circle! *(MR. and MRS. PORTER appear in the doorway DOWN RIGHT. Despite the heat, he wears a full suit and she wears a heavy, floor-length hoop skirt, white blouse, jacket, and hat. They both seem very upset.)*

MR. PORTER: Here he is! Doctor, I—!

MRS. PORTER: *(Panics.)* What's happened to my son?

MR. PORTER: He's not in his bed!

MRS. PORTER: Has something happened?

GORRIE: I apologize if we alarmed you, Mrs. Porter. Leonard was just here. A nurse is taking him back to his bed as we speak.

WARREN: *(Disapproves.)* By way of the garden!

MRS. PORTER: Oh, thank God!

MR. PORTER: *(To MRS. PORTER.)* I said there must be an explanation, my dear. Come and sit here. *(Brings her to a chair.)* You look faint.

MRS. PORTER: I'm all right, Henry. I want to see Leonard!

GORRIE: By all means, Mrs. Porter. Nurse Warren, will you see that Mr. and Mrs. Porter get to Leonard's ward safely?

WARREN: Certainly, Doctor. *(To the PORTERS.)* Come with me, please. *(Starts for the door.)*

MR. PORTER: *(To MRS. PORTER.)* You go on ahead, my dear. I'd like a few words with Dr. Gorrie. I'll join you shortly.

MRS. PORTER: If you say so, Henry.

WARREN: Right this way, Mrs. Porter. *(EXITS RIGHT with MRS. PORTER.)*

MR. PORTER: Well, Doctor? Is my son going to pull through?

GORRIE: I'm concerned about his fever. Leonard's a strong boy and a fighter. His chances of overcoming the malaria are encouraging. I was hoping that the cooling room would help, but I fear it was an experiment that has failed.

MR. PORTER: Cooling room? Where can you find such a thing in this heat?

GORRIE: It's right behind you, Mr. Porter. *(Points to the open doorway UP LEFT.)* Take a look.

MR. PORTER: *(EXITS LEFT briefly, then comes back ON.)* Feels pretty hot in there to me.

GORRIE: With the machine off and the door open, I'm sure it's stifling in there now. But earlier—

MR. PORTER: What's this machine? *(Goes over to the large machine where the cabinet doors are still wide open.)* Quite a contraption. What does it do?

GORRIE: The idea is to lower the temperature by removing the moisture from the air. The machine runs on steam, which is released up this pipe to the outside. The principle of the machine is based on the law of physics that… Oh, but I must be boring you with all this scientific—

MR. PORTER: I manufacture steam turbines. I'm interested. What law of physics?

GORRIE: The law that warm air rises and cold air descends. I built the room so that ice blocks could be placed above and the cool air would descend.

MR. PORTER: Where does the hot air go?

GORRIE: Out of vents placed in the ceiling. But I needed some kind of machine to force the cool air down and the hot air upwards. Of course, in this Florida weather, a block of ice, if you can get one, doesn't last very long. But I soon discovered that removing the water in the air—

MR. PORTER: The moisture!

GORRIE: Exactly! If I could reduce the humidity level, it would be easier to allow the cool air to dominate.

MR. PORTER: Fascinating.

GORRIE: Fascinating but ineffective. The malaria doesn't seem to be affected at all by the cooling room.

MR. PORTER: Well, it may not help stop malaria, Doctor, but you are doing something remarkable here.

GORRIE: In what way, Mr. Porter?

MR. PORTER: I'm a bit of an inventor myself, Dr. Gorrie. I have a few patents on turbines and such. But I'm also a businessman. You tell me you have a way of making a room cooler, and I say you've got something!

GORRIE: But medically, the cooling room has proven to be a failure.

MR. PORTER: Medically, maybe. But look beyond that. What do you call this contraption that cools this room?

GORRIE: An air conditioner. Because it changes the condition of the air.

MR. PORTER: If only you could get over the problem of the ice. You can't get your hands on ice very easily. Especially down here in the South.

GORRIE: Theoretically, this idea can work without ice.

MR. PORTER: Without ice?

GORRIE: Theoretically. By removing the humidity and creating, somehow, a compressed chemical that turns cold when it is released into the air—

MRS. PORTER: *(APPEARS in the doorway DOWN RIGHT.)* Henry! Leonard is anxious to see you!

MR. PORTER: Well, I'm anxious to see him. Let's go! *(Heads for the door.)*

GORRIE: I was telling your husband that Leonard is quite a fighter, Mrs. Porter. He just might pull through.

MRS. PORTER: Do you really think so, Doctor?

MR. PORTER: No promises, dear. But Dr. Gorrie says there is reason for hope.

MRS. PORTER: Thank goodness! Come along, Henry!

MR. PORTER: Yes, dear. *(To GORRIE.)* You keep working on that contraption of yours, Doctor. I think you've got something there.

MRS. PORTER: *(To MR. PORTER.)* What contraption? Honestly, Henry, you say the strangest things sometimes! *(The PORTERS EXIT RIGHT. After a pause, GORRIE crosses to the machine box and stares at it.)*

WARREN: *(ENTERS RIGHT.)* Should I get Johnny Wilkins ready for the cooling room, Doctor?

GORRIE: *(Thinks a moment.)* No, I don't think so. A waste of time, I'm afraid.

WARREN: *(Sad.)* As you say, Doctor. *(EXITS RIGHT.)*

GORRIE: *(Stares again at the machine.)* Without ice… It must be possible. *(LIGHTS FADE OUT.)*

AFTERMATH

Gorrie continued his experiments with refrigeration and took out a patent in 1851 on a machine that made ice. He was deeply involved in the invention of a refrigerated machine that worked without ice when he died at the age of fifty-two. His ideas and experiments later led to methods of refrigerating space, making Dr. John Gorrie the Father of Air Conditioning.

HER FIRST DECISION
(1863)

BACKGROUND

After much debate and months of political maneuvering, Abraham Lincoln signed the Emancipation Proclamation on January 1, 1863, thereby abolishing slavery in ten states. The Southern States, deep in a war against the Union, ignored the proclamation. But for the half million slaves in the North and those who escaped to the North, they were legally free.

SETTING

TIME: January 1863.
PLACE: The parlor of Mrs. Treadwell's home in Richmond, Virginia.

CHARACTERS

MRS. TREADWELL (F) .... mature widow
SERENA (F) .... black house slave

SET DESCRIPTION

The parlor is an elegant room with early Victorian style furnishings. There are two doors, one RIGHT and the other LEFT.

LIGHTS UP on MRS. TREADWELL, who still wears black fourteen years after her husband's death. She is standing at the RIGHT door, calling into another room.

MRS. TREADWELL: Lafayette! Lafayette! *(To herself.)* Where can that boy be! *(Shouts again.)* Lafayette!

SERENA: *(ENTERS through the LEFT door, wearing a simple but presentable servant's uniform.)* Mrs. Treadwell...

MRS. TREADWELL: Serena! Where is Lafayette?

SERENA: He gone, ma'am.

MRS. TREADWELL: Gone? Gone where? I didn't send him on any errands.

SERENA: No, ma'am. No errands.

MRS. TREADWELL: Where then?

SERENA: Just gone, ma'am.

MRS. TREADWELL: I want him to get the buggy out. I'm going to pay a call on Mrs. Parker.

SERENA: You best walk over to Mrs. Parker's place, ma'am. A nice day for walkin'.

MRS. TREADWELL: Don't be silly, Serena. Go find Lafayette and tell him I want the buggy right away.

SERENA: Lafayette ain't gonna get that buggy out no more. He gone. He ain't comin' back.

MRS. TREADWELL: You talk such nonsense, Serena! How do you know such a thing?

SERENA: 'Cause he told me so hisself, ma'am. Just afore he gone off.

MRS. TREADWELL: What are you talking about?

SERENA: Lafayette done leave us. Took his things and gone off early this mornin'.

MRS. TREADWELL: He's run off? Ridiculous! Lafayette might be a bit stubborn in his ways, but he's not the kind of slave to run away.

SERENA: Lafayette says he not a slave no more.

MRS. TREADWELL: Has that boy been drinking again?

SERENA: Not that I noticed.

MRS. TREADWELL: Then why is he acting so crazy? Run away? Stuff and nonsense! And at his age. Why he's sixty years old, if he's a day. He knows he can't get out of Richmond if I call the sheriff. What's got into him?

SERENA: It's this Proclamation, ma'am. It got all kinds of folks acting mighty strange.

MRS. TREADWELL: What Proclamation?

SERENA: Mister Lincoln's Proclamation, ma'am.

MRS. TREADWELL: Lincoln! Since when do we pay any attention to that man?

SERENA: Lafayette say it called the Emancipation Proclamation. Mr. Lincoln say all the slaves is now free.

MRS. TREADWELL: In the North, Serena! Not in the Confederacy.

SERENA: No, ma'am. Lafayette say Lincoln say all the slaves is free, North and South.

MRS. TREADWELL: Lafayette is talking nonsense. You sure he's not been drinking again?

SERENA: He as sober as can be when he told me this mornin'.

MRS. TREADWELL: What else did the fool boy tell you?

SERENA: About how there ain't no slavery no more, and if a Negro gonna work for somebody, that somebody's gotta pay him.

MRS. TREADWELL: Insolence!

SERENA: And he says now a Negro can go anywheres he wants to work 'cause he ain't nobody's property.

MRS. TREADWELL: I've never heard such talk! I'm going to send for the sheriff. Serena, you run on down to the City Hall and tell Sheriff O'Hara that my boy Lafayette has run off.

SERENA: Pardon, ma'am, but that won't do no good. They say hundreds of slaves gone run off since yesterday. I don't think Sheriff O'Hara gonna catch them all.

MRS. TREADWELL: What is going on?! Has everyone just gone and lost his head? Oh, how I wish my late husband was still alive. Dr. Treadwell would know what to do.

SERENA: It the Proclamation, ma'am. It called the Emancipation Proclamation, and it—

MRS. TREADWELL: I don't care if it's called the Second Coming! Just because that reprobate Lincoln says something or other is no reason for everybody to go crazy! Next thing you know, the cotton fields will be empty, and there will be no one left to cook and clean and—

SERENA: Lafayette say the Negro still gonna work. But for money. Not like slaves.

MRS. TREADWELL: Serena, I don't think I need hear any more of what Lafayette says. Such ideas!

SERENA: They ain't Lafayette's words, Mrs. Treadwell. It the Proclamation.

MRS. TREADWELL: Stop saying that!

SERENA: Sorry, ma'am.

MRS. TREADWELL: I hope you didn't pay no heed to what Lafayette was saying.

SERENA: No, ma'am. I mean...

MRS. TREADWELL: Serena?

SERENA: It just that... Lafayette say—

MRS. TREADWELL: *(Impatient.)* Serena!

SERENA: I mean, Mr. Lincoln say all the slaves is free now. Not just the menfolk.

MRS. TREADWELL: What are you trying to say, Serena?

SERENA: Ellie over at Mrs. Parker's place, she gone off last night. And Ruby that was with old Miss Donnelly gone off this mornin'.

MRS. TREADWELL: Foolish girls! They'll starve to death!

SERENA: And old Mammy down at the Harris house—the one is blind in one eye—she left, too.

MRS. TREADWELL: Mammy Wallace? Where is that old thing gonna get work? Mrs. Harris kept her on only because of the kindness of her Christian heart.

SERENA: What I heard is Mammy Wallace say she gonna die soon, and she wanna die a free woman.

MRS. TREADWELL: Insanity!

SERENA: I reckon Mr. Lincoln gone and started a heap of trouble for everybody.

MRS. TREADWELL: He certainly has, Serena. And I'm glad you see it that way.

SERENA: All the same, it make a body think.

MRS. TREADWELL: What?

SERENA: If Mr. Lincoln say—

MRS. TREADWELL: Lincoln is a fool!

SERENA: And if this Emancipation Proclamation say what it say—

MRS. TREADWELL: Yankee propaganda!

SERENA: Then maybe I ought to think things out.

MRS. TREADWELL: Think all you want, Serena, but don't lose your common sense.

SERENA: I been working for you ever since Dr. Treadwell bought me twenty-two years ago. And I reckon that a long time.

MRS. TREADWELL: And you've been happy here, haven't you, Serena?

SERENA: Happy? I don't rightly know what that mean.

MRS. TREADWELL: We've treated you fair. Never beat you or punished you like some do.

SERENA: That true enough.

MRS. TREADWELL: And you've had a nice place to live with your own room in the attic and such. And we took care of you, didn't we? Like that time you had the scarlet fever, and Dr. Treadwell gave you medicine.

SERENA: He did. I recall it well.

MRS. TREADWELL: Dr. Treadwell and I gave you a home. You'd best remember that, too.

SERENA: But this your house, Mrs. Treadwell. It ain't never been a home to me. Not my idea of home.

MRS. TREADWELL: You ungrateful girl!

SERENA: I reckon I am grateful, ma'am. Like you said, I got it better here than some do. But all the same, I gotta think it out for myself.

MRS. TREADWELL: Serena! Are you contemplating running off, too?

SERENA: Well...

MRS. TREADWELL: Don't you lie to me, Serena. You are a good Christian woman, even if you are a Negro, and you'd best tell me the truth!

SERENA: Well...

MRS. TREADWELL: Out with it, girl!

SERENA: I do confess I done decided to leave.

MRS. TREADWELL: *(Shocked.)* Serena! *(Pauses and considers the fact, then gets weak and panics.)* But what would I do? First Lafayette gone, and then you? How will I manage? How will I survive?

SERENA: You gonna survive fine, Mrs. Treadwell. You can get yourself a new girl. Won't have to buy a new slave. If you're willing to pay wages, you'll get someone else.

MRS. TREADWELL: *(Desperate.)* I don't want someone else! I want you to stay!

SERENA: No, ma'am.

MRS. TREADWELL: I'll pay you, Serena! Just like you said. I'll pay wages!

SERENA: That very kind of you, ma'am. But to me, it be just the same as afore. I reckon I best go off on my own and see what it like bein' a free woman.

MRS. TREADWELL: I'll tell you what it'll be like! It will be terrible! No place to live, no regular meals, no work, and no money. And even if you do find a job, it won't pay enough to live. You'll be worse off than you were when you were a slave!

SERENA: Maybe what you say is true. I don't rightly know. But I gotta try and see for myself.

MRS. TREADWELL: *(Angry.)* Well, don't you come crawling back to me when you find out what the real world is like!

SERENA: *(Hard.)* I promise I won't, ma'am.

MRS. TREADWELL: *(Softens.)* Serena, don't do anything until you think this thing through.

SERENA: I thought about it all last night. Hardly slept a wink. I figured I gots to make a decision. Mrs. Treadwell, I almost forty years old, and never afore in my life has I got to make a decision. All the time folks tellin' me what to do, where to live, what to cook, even what to think. I ain't never had to decide on anythin' by myself afore. And now, for the first time, I gots to make a big decision, and I didn't rightly know how to go about it. Then I says to myself, "Serena, now you gots a future. Ain't never had a future afore." If I stay here I won't ever get one. So I decided I gotta go.

MRS. TREADWELL: What good is a future of misery and poverty and—?

SERENA: Maybe it be like that, ma'am. Maybe not. I'll never know for sure if I stay here. *(Moves toward the door.)*

MRS. TREADWELL: Serena!

SERENA: *(Stops.)* Yes, ma'am?

MRS. TREADWELL: Where are you going?

SERENA: To fix supper. I got potatoes to peel and—

MRS. TREADWELL: But…

SERENA: Then after I wash them dishes and clean up some, I'm goin' upstairs and pack my things. I be gone afore you wake up tomorrow mornin'. *(EXITS LEFT.)*

MRS. TREADWELL: *(Calls after her, weak.)* Serena… *(To herself.)* What will I do? *(Frightened.)* What terrible thing have you done, Mr. Lincoln? *(LIGHTS FADE OUT.)*

AFTERMATH

Slavery continued in the South until the end of the Civil War in 1865. By that time, thousands of blacks had escaped from the South and found freedom in the North. Yet life was not easy for the newly freed slaves. Many faced unemployment, homelessness, and poverty.

LAURA KEENE'S BIG NIGHT
(1865)

BACKGROUND

When Confederate General Robert E. Lee surrendered unconditionally to the Union on April 12, 1865, there was a great deal of bitterness on the part of Southerners and Confederate sympathizers. The actor John Wilkes Booth was an avid pro-South activist and spearheaded a plot to assassinate President Abraham Lincoln as well as Secretary of State William H. Seward and Vice President Andrew Johnson all on the same night, thereby crippling the Union government. On the night of the planned assassinations, a gala performance of the comedy *Our American Cousin* was taking place at Ford's Theatre in Washington, DC, where actress-manager Laura Keene was to give her one-thousandth performance as the flighty comic character Florence Trenchard. Although it was Good Friday and many theatregoers thought it inappropriate to go to the theatre, Mr. and Mrs. Lincoln announced that they would attend the event.

SETTING

TIME: Friday, April 14, 1865.

PLACE: The backstage of Ford's Theatre in Washington, DC during a performance of the comedy *Our American Cousin.*

CHARACTERS

HARRY HAWK (M)..................... comedian

LAURA KEENE (F) .... famous actress-manager

JEANNIE GOURLAY (F)............. young actress in the company

E. A. SOTHERN (M).................... rising star; familiarly called "Eddie"

HELEN MUZZY (F)..................... experienced actress in the
                                  company
JOHN WILKES BOOTH (M)........ popular actor
UNION CAPTAIN (M).................. President Lincoln's guard
UNION OFFICER (M)................... another

SET DESCRIPTION

The action takes place in the STAGE RIGHT wing of the theatre. The stage is OFF LEFT, with dressing rooms and the stage door OFF RIGHT. The backstage area is littered with scenery and props.

PROPERTIES

Tray with tea items (HELEN MUZZY); pistol (JOHN WILKES BOOTH); weapons (UNION CAPTAIN, UNION OFFICER).

SOUND EFFECTS

Muffled audience laughter, band music for "Hail to the Chief," muffled applause, gunshot.

LIGHTS UP on the actor HARRY HAWK. He stands alone, watching and listening to the action happening on the Ford's Theatre stage OFF LEFT. He wears a somewhat flamboyant suit of the time, as befits the costume of a comic character. We hear MUFFLED AUDIENCE LAUGHTER, then LAURA KEENE ENTERS LEFT, coming from the stage. She is dressed as an aristocratic lady of the day.

HARRY: Well, this is your big night, Mrs. Keene. Is it really the one-thousandth time you are playing Florence Trenchard? Or did you make the numbers up?

LAURA: It is indeed my one-thousandth performance. I keep an accurate count. Since I first played Mrs. Trenchard in 1858, I have reprised the role 999 times.

HARRY: *(Sly.)* Including that week in Pittsburgh during Lent when no one came?

LAURA: Don't be impudent, Mr. Hawk. *(Pause.)* I had a good audience on that Wednesday.

HARRY: The matinee. How's the house tonight?

LAURA: Sold out, but you have to squeeze the laughs out of them. Everyone keeps looking at the presidential box, wondering when Mr. Lincoln is going to arrive.

HARRY: Still not here?

LAURA: He's usually late, but not this late. Outrageous!

HARRY: Maybe he's not coming.

LAURA: Oh, he'll come, all right. Mr. Lincoln never misses a comedy, if he can help it. It's the tragedies he doesn't like. Not once has he seen my Lady Macbeth!

HARRY: I read that Honest Abe prefers to read tragedies than see them.

LAURA: Honest Abe! Show some respect, Harry Hawk! He is the President!

HARRY: President or hick lawyer, he likes a good laugh. Maybe now he'll have more opportunity for laughter.

LAURA: With the war over, I wonder if the company should tour the South again. Charleston used to love me. And Savannah, too.

HARRY: It's your company. Now you can go anywhere you want. How about New Orleans?

LAURA: A terrible theatre town. Always was and always will be.

HARRY: *(Laughs.)* Just because they booed your Juliet—

LAURA: My Juliet has never been booed!

HARRY: I beg your pardon, Mrs. Keene. Maybe it was your Portia! *(Laughs.)*

LAURA: Sometimes, Mr. Hawk, you are insufferable!

JEANNIE: *(ENTERS RIGHT from the dressing rooms and joins them. She is wearing an upper-class dress of a young aristocrat of the day and carries a fan.)* Is the President here yet?

HARRY: Not quite, Jeannie.

JEANNIE: I hope he shows up. I've never acted for a president before.

HARRY: *(Smiles.)* I thought you played Puck for Jefferson Davis.

JEANNIE: Really, Mr. Hawk! Just because I'm from Maryland!

LAURA: Behave yourself, Mr. Hawk. Save your comedics for the stage.

HARRY: *(Mocks.)* Oh! But if only they would let me play Hamlet!

LAURA: Hush! I want to check on this scene. *(They all look OFF LEFT. SOUND EFFECT: MUFFLED AUDIENCE LAUGHTER.)*

JEANNIE: Oh, Mr. Sothern is so funny in this scene.

LAURA: He's overplaying it again.

HARRY: Laying it on thick, you might say.

LAURA: The way he's carrying on, one would think we are celebrating his one-thousandth performance.

JEANNIE: Oh, he's too young for that!

LAURA: I beg your pardon?

JEANNIE: Oh, I didn't mean—

HARRY: Isn't that your cue, Jeannie?

JEANNIE: What? Oh! It is! *(Rushes OFF LEFT.)*

HARRY: Sweet girl. Young... but sweet.

LAURA: Indeed.

HELEN: *(ENTERS LEFT from the stage. She is in her forties and dressed as a servant, carrying a tray with tea items.)* Everybody in the audience keeps looking at the President's box. Some of them are going to end up with a stiff neck!

LAURA: He's never been this late.

HELEN: Not that I can recall. Mr. Lincoln likes his comedies, they say.

HARRY: Perhaps he is too tired to go to the theatre. After all, he's just won a war. Very exhausting winning a war, they tell me.

LAURA: Mr. Hawk, if you cannot speak with respect regarding Mr.— *(SOUND EFFECT: BAND MUSIC "Hail to the Chief" plays. SOUND EFFECT: MUFFLED APPLAUSE. The three of them rush LEFT to watch OFF LEFT.)*

HELEN: It's him!

LAURA: And about time, too!

HARRY: Honest Abe in all his glory!

HELEN: My, but he is tall indeed!

HARRY: Gets taller every time I see him. *(The MUSIC ENDS and the APPLAUSE tapers off.)*

LAURA: Now get on with the play!

HARRY: That took the wind out of Eddie's sails.

HELEN: Has he forgotten his lines?

HARRY: No. Just flustered. You know how Eddie hates it when someone steps on his line.

LAURA: *(To OFF LEFT.)* Carry on, you ham, you!

HELEN: There he goes. He's back on track again.

HARRY: Poor Eddie. Upstaged by the President of the United States! He'll never live this down.

JEANNIE: *(ENTERS LEFT from the stage.)* I saw him! Honest Abe, as big as life!

LAURA: That was no reason to gawk, Jeannie. After all, we are professionals.

JEANNIE: I was waiting for Eddie to say his line.

HARRY: Uh-oh. Here he comes! *(E. A. SOTHERN, a dashing actor, ENTERS LEFT in a furious temper. He wears a dark and well-tailored suit with a lace cravat.)*

EDDIE: Of all the disrespectful behavior! I've never been so insulted in all my life!

HARRY: Oh, yes, you have.

EDDIE: Right in the middle of my best speech! He could have had the decency to wait until the first intermission!

HARRY: And miss my best scene? I should hope not!

EDDIE: I tried to continue after the rude interruption, but my rhythm was off. I couldn't get the audience back. Some of my best laugh lines—lost forever!

LAURA: Mr. Sothern, your performance tonight is overwrought and embarrassing! You are delivering your lines like a carnival barker!

21

EDDIE: I am giving the exact same performance I give every night! But this audience is so unresponsive, I have to work all the harder.

LAURA: That scene with the reverend was outrageous!

EDDIE: Don't you know high comedy when you see it?

LAURA: High comedy? That?

JEANNIE: Mrs. Keene! Mr. Hawk! We're on!

LAURA: I'll speak with you later, Mr. Sothern!

JEANNIE: Hurry! *(EXITS LEFT with LAURA and HARRY.)*

EDDIE: I say this play is an insult to my talent!

HELEN: *Our American Cousin?* It's a grand, old comedy. Always brings them in. I remember once in Minneapolis, it was a blizzard outside, and still they came.

EDDIE: I swear, someday I shall do nothing but Shakespeare!

HELEN: You'll starve.

EDDIE: And no out-of-date managers like Laura Keene! I think the theatre should be modern!

HELEN: Modern? Like Shakespeare?

EDDIE: Away with the old! In with the new!

HELEN: You'll starve for sure.

JEANNIE: *(ENTERS LEFT.)* I saw Mr. Lincoln laugh!

HELEN: He likes his comedies, all right. Always has.

JEANNIE: This is so exciting! Isn't it, Mr. Sothern? Acting for the President of the United States!

EDDIE: I don't think theatre should mix with politics.

LAURA: *(ENTERS LEFT.)* And another thing, Mr. Sothern—!

EDDIE: My cue, I think. *(EXITS LEFT.)*

LAURA: That man is so infuriating!

JEANNIE: But so handsome—er, I mean, funny. On stage, that is.

HELEN: You've seen one good-looking ham, you've seen them all.

JEANNIE: Mrs. Keene, I saw Mr. Lincoln laugh!

LAURA: Hush! I want to hear what kind of laugh the "sockdologizing old man-trap" line gets.

HELEN: Oh, they always laugh at that line, Mrs. Keene.

LAURA: Not always. But I know for a fact Mr. Lincoln finds it amusing. Listen… *(A pause, then SOUND EFFECT: MUFFLED AUDIENCE LAUGHTER followed by SOUND EFFECT: GUNSHOT.)* What was that?!

JOHN WILKES BOOTH: *(From OFF LEFT.) Sic semper tyrannis!*

JEANNIE: That's not in the play!

LAURA: That's not Harry! Or Mr. Sothern! *(JOHN WILKES BOOTH rushes ON LEFT with a pistol in his hand, limping.)*

JEANNIE: Johnny Booth!

LAURA: Wilkes! What are you doing on my stage?

BOOTH: The South is avenged! Out of my way, you silly cow! *(Pushes past LAURA and runs OFF RIGHT.)*

HARRY: *(ENTERS LEFT with EDDIE.)* He just shot the President!

LAURA: What?!

HARRY: Then he jumped from the box onto the stage! *(The UNION CAPTAIN and the UNION OFFICER run ON LEFT with weapons drawn.)*

CAPTAIN: Where is he?!

JEANNIE: *(Points RIGHT.)* He ran off that way! Through the stage door!

LAURA: Shot the President?!

CAPTAIN: *(To the OFFICER.)* After him! I'll cover the side alley!

OFFICER: Yes, Captain! *(EXITS RIGHT.)*

LAURA: I don't understand… shot the President? During my performance?

CAPTAIN: No one move. The theatre is surrounded! *(Starts to EXIT LEFT.)*

EDDIE: I saw it all, Captain!

HARRY: So did I! (Starts to follow.)

CAPTAIN: Stay right where you are. You're all under arrest! *(EXITS LEFT.)*

HELEN: What did he say?

LAURA: *(Numb.)* Mr. Lincoln shot during my performance?

EDDIE: Under arrest! This is outrageous!

HARRY: Well, Mrs. Keene, your one-thousandth performance has sure turned out to be a memorable one after all. *(BLACKOUT.)*

AFTERMATH

Laura Keene and all members of the company were arrested and held in jail until it was determined that they were not among Booth's conspirators. The theatre company went bankrupt, Mrs. Keene suffered a nervous breakdown, and her career never recovered. She died twenty-eight years later a broken woman. E. A. Sothern went on to have a long and distinguished career in the theatre. As for Ford's Theatre, it was closed right after the assassination, and the building was used for various purposes over the decades. A play would not be performed again at Ford's until 1968, over one hundred years later.

THE GOOD FIGHT
(1873)

BACKGROUND

Two of the most prominent leaders of the women's suffrage movement in the nineteenth century were Susan B. Anthony and Elizabeth Cady Stanton. They were first active as abolitionists in the anti-slavery movement during the Civil War and then became major spokespersons for the women's right to vote. They gave speeches, wrote books, and created organizations that pushed for women's suffrage. In 1872 in Rochester, New York, Susan B. Anthony attempted to vote in the national election. She was arrested and fined, but she refused to pay. Her case went to trial in 1873 at the regional Federal Circuit Court in Canandaigua, New York, where she was found guilty and fined one hundred dollars. Not allowed to testify at her own trial, Anthony was asked by Justice Ward Hunt if she had anything to say before the sentencing. Anthony then delivered one of the most elegant and persuasive speeches in the history of women's rights. Refusing to pay the fine, she was sentenced to prison until she paid.

SETTING

TIME: June 18, 1873.

PLACE: A room in the federal circuit courthouse in Canandaigua, New York.

CHARACTERS

ELIZABETH CADY
     STANTON (F).........................suffragette; 58 years old
HENRY R. SELDEN (M) ....defense attorney
SUSAN B. ANTHONY (F)............suffragette; 52 years old
PRISON MATRON (F) ....in Anthony's prison

SET DESCRIPTION

The room is sparsely furnished with a few chairs and a table. A single door leads to the hallway OFF LEFT. There is a large window and a portrait of George Washington on the wall.

LIGHTS UP on ELIZABETH CADY STANTON and HENRY R. SELDEN alone in the room. He wears a period three-piece suit, and she wears a full-length dark dress and a dark hat with a veil. Both are anxious and pacing about.

STANTON: You don't think they will bring her directly to the jail, do you, Mr. Selden?

SELDEN: Not at all customary. The prisoner must have access to counsel in case there is an issue of bail.

STANTON: Prisoner! I wish you wouldn't use that term.

SELDEN: Just legal terminology, Mrs. Stanton.

STANTON: And accurate, I'm afraid.

SELDEN: Of course, Miss Anthony need not go to prison. She was found guilty of trying to vote in a national election, and that is not a penal crime. The sentencing stated only a fine.

STANTON: If I know Susan—and I have for several years—she won't pay the one hundred dollars or accept bail.

SELDEN: I tend to agree with you, sad to say.

STANTON: But she'll say it was all worth it. Her speech in court was superb! Even Justice Hunt seemed bamboozled by it.

SELDEN: Had there been a jury, they would have been overwhelmed.

STANTON: No jury—and they call that American justice!

SELDEN: Federal Circuit Courts are different from regular courts, Mrs. Stanton.

STANTON: I fear that Susan's powerful words fell on deaf ears this afternoon.

SELDEN: Not completely. The newspapermen heard her and, given the notoriety of this case, they will give it thorough coverage in their papers.

STANTON: Which papers were here?

SELDEN: Well, the Canandaigua one, for sure.

STANTON: That is what they call "small potatoes," I believe?

SELDEN: Not a large readership, no. I recognized the editor from the Rochester paper. And probably Buffalo was here as well.

STANTON: No New York City newspapers? Or Washington or Boston?

SELDEN: *(Hesitant.)* I… I don't think so.

STANTON: The whole country should be reading what Susan said today. "Laws are made by men, under a government of men, interpreted by men for the benefit of men. The only chance women have for justice is to violate the law, as I have done, and I shall continue to do so!"

SELDEN: You have quite a memory, Mrs. Stanton.

STANTON: Oh, Susan has said it many times before. Just not as elegantly and passionately as she did today.

SELDEN: As a spokesperson, Miss Anthony is quite persuasive. But as a client, she can be very infuriating. I wished she had taken my advice on several matters.

STANTON: Not Susan. She runs her own show. You, Mr. Selden, were just a formality that the law required.

SELDEN: Well, she'll need my help now if she wants to stay out of jail.

STANTON: I wonder... *(The PRISON MATRON ENTERS LEFT with ANTHONY through the door. MATRON wears a simple gray uniform dress. ANTHONY is dressed formally in dark colors and wears her hair in a tight bun.)*

STANTON: Susan! You were magnificent! *(Embraces her formally.)*

ANTHONY: Thank you, Mrs. Stanton. I shall hazard a guess that Mr. Selden was not similarly impressed.

SELDEN: A fine speech, Miss Anthony. No question about it. But—

ANTHONY: But not according to protocol. Well, I had only one opportunity to speak, and I used it.

STANTON: You certainly did that!

SELDEN: Matron, what are your instructions?

MATRON: I am to remain with the prisoner in here while we await orders from Justice Hunt.

STANTON: Orders? I thought the trial and the sentencing were over.

SELDEN: They are, Mrs. Stanton. But the court is allowed to deliberate some before a formal decision is made.

ANTHONY: I think the Justice needs a bit of time to cool off some.

SELDEN: He is probably saying the same thing about you, Miss Anthony.

ANTHONY: No doubt! *(Laughs with STANTON.)* Well, I'm in no hurry to go to jail. I'll give him his thinking time.

SELDEN: It will come to you as no surprise that I strongly urge you to pay the one hundred dollars and go free.

ANTHONY: Free? How little freedom women actually have in this country, Mr. Selden. Thank the Lord that I am unmarried. If I were, my husband would pay the fine and tell me to shut up! As I am not wed, I am actually a little more free, as you say, than most women. At least I can make my own decisions.

SELDEN: But for a matter of only one hundred dollars—

ANTHONY: Only? Stop thinking like a lawyer, Mr. Selden. I don't have one hundred dollars. In fact, my legal fees and debts are now close to ten thousand dollars!

STANTON: *(Concerned.)* And where does an unmarried woman come by that much money?

ANTHONY: *(Flippant.)* I will gradually pay it off through speaking engagements, pamphlets, books, and taking in washing!

SELDEN: *(Serious.)* That will be difficult to do from a prison cell.

ANTHONY: True. But a woman in prison really doesn't have to worry about money, does she?

SELDEN: *(Impatient.)* Miss Anthony, you are infuriating!

ANTHONY: *(Sincere.)* I'm sorry to upset you so, Mr. Selden. I do believe you are more disturbed by the situation than I am.

SELDEN: *(Pouts.)* I hate to see justice abused.

ANTHONY: Abused by whom? Justice Hunt or myself?

SELDEN: *(Defeated.)* I am sure there will be no difficulty in raising the one hundred dollars—these women's organizations and such. You are a much-admired woman, Miss Anthony.

STANTON: But most of her admirers are women.

ANTHONY: Thank you for the suggestion, Mr. Selden, but I have a plan of my own. And I might need your help.

SELDEN: I'm afraid to ask…

STANTON: I'm not. What's your plan, Susan?

ANTHONY: It's a very legal one. Since I have been found guilty by a federal circuit court, my only alternative in getting justice is to go to the Supreme Court in Washington.

STANTON: Of course!

ANTHONY: Even if I lose my case there, I will have the whole nation's attention. I can do more good for women's suffrage by going to the Supreme Court and failing than I could have by winning this case here in Canandaigua.

SELDEN: But the Supreme Court…!

ANTHONY: The big show, Mr. Selden. Are you up to it?

SELDEN: *(Befuddled.)* I… I… I don't know what to say.

ANTHONY: Don't say anything now, Mr. Selden. Just think about it.

SELDEN: It's an awfully big step...

STANTON: Susan only takes big steps. Always has.

SELDEN: And the expense...

ANTHONY: Oh, I will have no trouble getting help to go into deeper debt.

STANTON: I will start a fundraising campaign right away! Women everywhere will want to help!

SELDEN: Ten thousand dollars plus? I doubt that very much.

STANTON: Don't underestimate American women, Mr. Selden. *(To MATRON.)* What do you think, Matron? Would you contribute a little something to Miss Anthony's cause?

MATRON: *(Surprised.)* Me?

STANTON: You're a working woman. What are your feelings?

MATRON: But my job is to put her in jail!

STANTON: And I'm sure you will do an excellent job of it when the time comes. But for Miss Anthony to get to the Supreme Court, we need to raise money.

ANTHONY: I wouldn't dream of taking money from my dear Matron. Why, she only earns— *(To MATRON.)* May I ask how much you earn, Madam Matron?

MATRON: Three dollars and eighty cents a month.

ANTHONY: *(To STANTON.)* Only three dollars and eighty cents a month.

MATRON: The men over at the penitentiary get three times that much!

ANTHONY: I am not surprised. *(To SELDEN.)* Are you, Mr. Selden?

MATRON: But I can give you a little bit each month. Say fifteen cents?

ANTHONY: You are a dear, Madam Matron. But I couldn't take one cent.

SELDEN: This is all ridiculous! I'm going back into court to see what is going on with Justice Hunt! *(Starts for the door.)*

ANTHONY: Give him my compliments!

SELDEN: Totally ridiculous! *(EXITS LEFT.)*

ANTHONY: Poor Mr. Selden. I don't think he has the courage to go to the Supreme Court. Do you, Mrs. Stanton?

STANTON: He's a good lawyer, I suppose, but not man enough for what we need.

ANTHONY: What do you think, Madam Matron?

MATRON: Me?

ANTHONY: Of course you.

MATRON: Well... I think he's afraid of his own shadow. I'll bet he's got a wife who keeps a heavy thumb on him.

STANTON: I wouldn't be surprised.

ANTHONY: The only thing worse than men who hate women are those who are afraid of them. Like Justice Hunt in there. Afraid of women speaking out. Afraid of women voting. Just plain afraid. Mrs. Stanton, we are fighting a war in which the enemy is afraid of us, so they fight all the harder.

MATRON: I hope you don't have to go to the women's prison, Miss Anthony. It ain't a nice place. You talk about how men behave and all, but there are some women in that place that are even worse, take my word for it.

STANTON: *(To MATRON.)* While we are waiting to go to the Supreme Court, will Miss Anthony have to remain in jail?

MATRON: Can't say. I'm no lawyer. *(SELDEN ENTERS LEFT.)*

ANTHONY: Let's ask this one.

SELDEN: I have good news, ladies!

STANTON: Yes?

SELDEN: Justice Hunt has suspended the one hundred dollar fine. You are free to go.

ANTHONY: He changed his mind?

SELDEN: Not totally. You are still found guilty of trying to vote, but there is no sentence.

ANTHONY: That means...?

SELDEN: It means the case is closed.

ANTHONY: Which means...?

SELDEN: You cannot take your case to a higher court.

STANTON: No Supreme Court?

SELDEN: No Supreme Court. *(To SUSAN.)* So, my defense duties as assigned to me by the State of New York are officially over. Good day to you, Miss Anthony... and Mrs. Stanton... and goodbye to you both. *(Starts to leave.)* Matron, you are no longer in charge of Miss Anthony and are to report to the court bailiff.

MATRON: Yes, sir. *(SELDEN EXITS LEFT.)* That's real good news, Miss Anthony. If you ever get in trouble again, remember my fifteen cents a month.

ANTHONY: Thank you, Matron. *(MATRON EXITS LEFT.)* Mrs. Stanton, we won and we lost.

STANTON: That's one way of looking at it. At least you are free to join me and the movement again. We need you, Susan.

ANTHONY: Continue the good fight for another year... or years.

STANTON: Maybe years. But we knew that from the start. Look how long it took us to get slavery abolished.

ANTHONY: And that took a war. It would be better if this fight doesn't take a war. Much better. *(They stand in silence as the LIGHTS FADE TO BLACK.)*

AFTERMATH

After the trial, Anthony and Stanton worked with Senator Aaron A. Sargent on a new bill, and in 1878, he introduced to Congress an amendment to the U. S. Constitution giving women the right to vote. The amendment was considered, neglected, and reviewed for many years. In 1920, the Nineteenth Amendment was finally passed, giving voting privileges to all female American citizens. Anthony and Stanton never stopped fighting for women's rights, but neither lived to see their dream become a reality. Stanton died in 1902 and Anthony in 1906.

BREAKER BOY
(1888)

BACKGROUND

Between 1880 and 1920, the coal industry in Pennsylvania relied on child labor to increase productivity and profits. At the age of eight, boys were hired for the "coal breaker room"—a dusty, enclosed space where nuggets of stone and coal poured in and the young workers had to pick out the coal pieces before the rest went down a chute. Bending over and breathing coal dust for ten hours a day left many of the youths with asthma and disfigured backs. At the age of fourteen, boys could join the adult workers in the mines, which were also dangerous and unhealthy. Many of the Pennsylvania coal miners were immigrants from Eastern Europe who settled in the hillside towns because of work opportunities in the mines.

SETTING

TIME: February 1888.
PLACE: The main room in the house of a Polish family in the rural town of Carbondale, Pennsylvania.

CHARACTERS

STANISLAW (M)........................... miner
IRINA (F) .... his pregnant wife
ANNA (F)...................................... their ten-year-old daughter
TOMASZ (M)................................ their eight-year-old son

SET DESCRIPTION

There is a wood burning stove UP RIGHT with a coffee pot, a pot of boiling water, a small pot of oatmeal, and two raw, unpeeled potatoes. A table with a coffee cup, bowl, and spoon sits LEFT with four chairs surrounding it. A cupboard stands UP CENTER with two pieces of cloth inside. A washbasin with a pump sits next to the stove RIGHT, and an oil lamp hangs from the low ceiling. There is a door RIGHT to the outside and another door LEFT to the bedroom. Coats and caps are hanging on hooks on the wall.

PROPERTIES

Boots, socks (TOMASZ).

LIGHTS UP on IRINA at the stove, where a pot of water is boiling next to a coffee pot and a small pot of oatmeal. It is just before dawn. She wears a worn, but heavy, dress and apron, and she is clearly pregnant. She takes two raw, unpeeled potatoes and drops them into the boiling water. STANISLAW ENTERS LEFT from the bedroom. He wears thick work pants and a shirt, both worn and faded.

STANISLAW: Did the boy eat something?

IRINA: A little oatmeal. He's too nervous. He says nothing, but I can tell.

STANISLAW: It's nearly dawn. We must be going soon.

IRINA: Is he dressed?

STANISLAW: Almost. I made him put on two pairs of socks.

IRINA: Is it cold in the breaker room?

STANISLAW: I don't know from experience. They say the boys keep warm by working.

IRINA: Bending and scrambling for bits of coal all day. Keeping your hands safe from the chute. I hear stories. And I see the breaker boys at church on Sundays. They are all stooped over like old men. And always coughing. Why are we doing this to little Tomasz?

STANISLAW: You know very well. Eighty-two cents a week. We need the money.

IRINA: Stanislaw, he is only eight years old. And so thin!

STANISLAW: With the money he earns, we can get better food. Then he won't be so thin. Are the potatoes ready?

IRINA: *(Checks the stove.)* In a few minutes.

STANISLAW: Then I have time for coffee?

IRINA: There is a little left. *(STANISLAW sits at the table. IRINA gets the coffee pot and pours a little into a cup on the table.)* I don't see why Tomasz must begin to work so young. Maybe wait a year—

STANISLAW: *(Impatient.)* Irina, we've been through all this before. The boy has to work.

IRINA: *(Sits at the table.)* Stanislaw, last night I had a dream about little Jozef.

STANISLAW: You shouldn't dwell on such things.

IRINA: I dreamt he was still alive. And it was his eighth birthday—

STANISLAW: The boy was only five when he died.

IRINIA: But in my dream he was just turning eight. And I kept saying to myself, "Soon he will be gone. Soon he will be sent to the breaker room."

STANISLAW: Irina...

IRINA: Then I woke up, and I realized it was all a dream. I was so relieved. Then I remembered that today Tomasz was to start work. My nightmare had come true!

STANISLAW: Such thinking only makes things worse. If you behave like that in front of the boy, he'll—

IRINA: Hush! He's coming. *(ANNA ENTERS LEFT, wearing a worn nightgown and heavy socks.)* Anna! What are you doing awake? It's too early.

ANNA: I heard talking. And I wanted to wish Tomasz good luck on his first day of work.

STANISLAW: *(To IRINA.)* That is the kind of attitude you must have. *(To ANNA.)* Come here, my girl, and sit on your papa's lap a moment before I have to go.

ANNA: *(Gets on his lap.)* Can I have a kiss?

STANISLAW: Of course you can, little one. There is no coal dust on my face now. Good time for a kiss! *(Kisses her cheek twice.)*

IRINA: *(Calls OFF LEFT into the bedroom.)* Tomasz! What is keeping you?

ANNA: Papa, why can't Tomasz work with you in the mine?

STANISLAW: Not until he is fourteen. Until then, he works in the breaker room.

ANNA: Nadia's brother works in the breaker room. She says it is a terrible place.

STANISLAW: You tell Nadia to mind her own business.

IRINA: Hush! He's coming! *(TOMASZ ENTERS LEFT, wearing a shirt and thick trousers that seem a little big for him. He carries a pair of boots.)* Here's my boy! What have you been up to?

TOMASZ: Papa said to put on two pairs of socks. But now I can't get the boots on. They're too tight.

IRINA: Let me help you. Sit here. *(TOMASZ sits at the table, and IRINA struggles to get the boots on.)*

STANISLAW: Look at your brave brother, Anna. Today he becomes a breaker boy!

IRINA: You have outgrown these boots, Tomasz. You better take off one pair of socks.

TOMASZ: All right. *(Pulls off the outer pair of socks.)*

STANISLAW: Now that you are a breaker boy, we can maybe afford a bigger pair of boots for you.

TOMASZ: Really, Papa? Mama?

IRINA: We shall see. *(Helps him put the boots on.)*

ANNA: Nadia's brother got new boots. His feet are huge! Like Papa's!

IRINA: How old is Nadia's brother?

ANNA: Nine, I think.

IRINA: I will have to talk to Nadia's mother. Maybe we can buy the old boots from her. Stand up, Tomasz, and let me see. *(He stands.)* Still too tight?

TOMASZ: Not too tight.

IRINA: Good. *(Looks at the socks he took off.)* These socks need darning again. I'll work on them today.

STANISLAW: Are the potatoes ready yet?

IRINA: Let me check. *(Goes to the stove and pokes a fork into the pot.)*

ANNA: Do breaker boys have time to eat a potato?

STANISLAW: They get a lunch break, just like the miners.

IRINA: They're ready. *(Pulls the two potatoes out of the pot with a fork and puts them on the table.)*

ANNA: I would like to be a breaker boy if I got to eat a whole potato for lunch!

IRINA: Don't talk nonsense, Anna. *(Goes to the cupboard and pulls out two pieces of cloth.)*

TOMASZ: Girls can't be breaker boys! Everyone knows that.

STANISLAW: *(To ANNA.)* What would you do with a whole potato?

ANNA: I'd eat it all!

IRINA: I'll wrap these up while they are still hot. *(Wraps each potato tightly in a cloth.)*

STANISLAW: *(To TOMASZ.)* Smells good, doesn't it? But do not eat it until the foreman says it is time for lunch. Understand?

TOMASZ: Yes, Papa.

IRINA: *(Gives TOMASZ his potato.)* Put it under your shirt. It will stay warmer that way.

TOMASZ: Yes, Mama. *(Tucks the wrapped potato in his shirt.)*

IRINA: Here is yours, Stanislaw. *(Hands him a wrapped potato.)*

STANISLAW: *(Rises and puts his potato inside his shirt.)* Time to go. *(Gets his coat and cap off the hook, while IRINA gets Tomasz's coat and cap and brings them to him.)*

IRINA: Here you are, my little worker. *(Helps him put on his coat.)*

ANNA: Not "little worker," Mama. Breaker boy!

STANISLAW: That's the right attitude! Come, Tomasz. It's beginning to get light. We don't want to be late.

TOMASZ: Goodbye, Mama.

IRINA: *(Hugs him.)* Goodbye, Tomasz. Be a good boy. Talk politely to the foreman.

STANISLAW: The foreman won't know any Polish. Best not to say anything.

ANNA: Goodbye, Tomasz! *(Gives him a quick hug.)*

STANISLAW: We will see you both tonight.

ANNA: I will help Mama heat up extra hot water for your washing, so there is enough water for both of you!

STANISLAW: You do that, Anna. And mind your mama today. You will have to do some of Tomasz's chores.

ANNA: Yes, Papa.

IRINA: *(As STANISLAW and TOMASZ EXIT RIGHT.)* Goodbye! Goodbye! *(They are gone.)*

ANNA: I'm hungry.

IRINA: There is a little oatmeal left. *(Goes toward the stove, but stops suddenly.)* Oh, my!

ANNA: What is it, Mama?

IRINA: The little one inside...

ANNA: The baby?

IRINA: He likes to kick.

ANNA: Does it hurt?

IRINA: *(Smiles.)* No, Anna. *(Continues to the stove.)*

ANNA: Why do you always say "he"? *(Sits at the table.)*

IRINA: I don't know. *(Dishes out the last of the oatmeal into a bowl on the table.)* Maybe because your Papa would like the baby to be a boy.

ANNA: What if it's a girl?

IRINA: He will love her just like he loves you.

ANNA: But do you want the baby to be a boy?

IRINA: I don't know. Eat your oatmeal while it is still hot.

ANNA: I can't decide if I want a baby brother or a baby sister. *(Eats.)*

IRINA: God will decide. *(Sits at the table, weary.)* But maybe if both you and I pray to God for you to have a baby sister, it would be best.

ANNA: Really?

IRINA: Just don't tell your Papa. Our secret.

ANNA: All right. *(Continues eating. LIGHTS FADE OUT.)*

AFTERMATH

Although Pennsylvania passed a law in 1885 forbidding children under fourteen from working in the coal mines, the law was not enforced very strongly. By 1910, machinery was used to separate coal and stone, and the job of "breaker boy" was abandoned, although pre-teen and teenage boys continued to work in the mines. Federal laws forbidding the employment of children in coal mines did not come about until the 1930s.

BEADED SOUVENIRS FOR SALE

(1891)

BACKGROUND

On December 29, 1890, the United States 7th Cavalry Regiment in South Dakota was ordered to go to Wounded Knee Creek and disarm the Native American tribe known as the Lakota. About 300 Lakota men, women, and children were camped there on reservation land. As the Lakota men were turning over their rifles to the soldiers, a deaf tribesman didn't understand why an officer tried to take his gun away. The two men struggled over the rifle, inciting some of the Lakota still armed to fire at the militia. The battle that ensued was more of a massacre, with over 260 Lakota men, women, and children killed. Of the 500 U. S. soldiers present, only twenty-five died in the fray. A three-day blizzard followed, after which the frozen bodies of the dead Lakotas were buried by the military in a mass grave. A Court of Inquiry looked into the incident, and all of the Union officers were exonerated. Twenty of the cavalry members received the Congressional Medal of Honor.

SETTING

TIME: February 1891.

PLACE: The interior of a Lakota teepee located near Wounded Knee Creek in South Dakota.

CHARACTERS

SPOTTED DEER (F) .... Lakota girl
BRAVE SPARROW (F) .... her mother
GRAY CLOUD (F) .... Spotted Deer's adult sister

BLIND OWL (F) .... elderly Lakota woman
WHITE HORSE (M) .... Brave Sparrow's husband

SET DESCRIPTION

The inside of the teepee has a small fire burning CENTER. A flap to the outside is RIGHT. Beaded belts, pouches, and jewelry are hanging from the teepee walls.

PROPERTIES

Needle, thread, beads, fabric, blankets (BRAVE SPARROW, SPOTTED DEER, GRAY CLOUD); blanket, walking stick (BLIND OWL).

SOUND EFFECTS

Horses approaching.

LIGHTS UP on BRAVE SPARROW and her two daughters, SPOTTED DEER and GRAY CLOUD, sitting around the small fire CENTER. ALL are in native dress, wrapped in blankets, and sewing beads onto pieces of fabric. Some completed belts, pouches, and jewelry are hanging from the teepee walls. They work quietly except for a low humming chant coming from BRAVE SPARROW.

SPOTTED DEER: Is this tight enough, Mother? *(Hands her cloth to BRAVE SPARROW.)*

BRAVE SPARROW: Tighter, little one. As tight as you can pull. *(Gives her back the beaded cloth.)*

SPOTTED DEER: But my fingers are so cold!

GRAY CLOUD: Pulling tighter will warm them, Spotted Deer.

BRAVE SPARROW: Do as your sister tells you.

BLIND OWL: *(OFF RIGHT.)* Brave Sparrow! Are you in there?

GRAY CLOUD: It sounds like Blind Owl.

BRAVE SPARROW: *(Rises.)* She should not be out in this cold. *(Opens the flap to the teepee.)* I am here, Blind Owl. Come inside and sit by the fire.

BLIND OWL: You have a fire? I cannot see the smoke.

BRAVE SPARROW: *(Helps BLIND OWL into the teepee.)* This way. Take my hand. *(BLIND OWL also has a blanket wrapped around her and uses a walking stick. She is mostly but not entirely blind. BRAVE SPARROW helps her sit by the fire.)*

BLIND OWL: Who do I see here? Gray Cloud! I can see you. And the other?

SPOTTED DEER: Spotted Deer.

BLIND OWL: Spotted Deer! The gods bless you, my little one. *(To BRAVE SPARROW.)* You have both of your daughters back with you now? That is good.

BRAVE SPARROW: Gray Cloud is alone now, so she has returned to her home.

BLIND OWL: I cannot see what you are doing. Not cooking. I cannot smell any cooking.

BRAVE SPARROW: What food is there to cook? No, Blind Owl, not cooking.

BLIND OWL: When I was born many, many moons ago, my father looked at my eyes, which were dark like clouds, and he named me Blind Owl. I was not actually blind then. But my father knew

I was clever. That is why he named me Blind Owl. My gift was wisdom, not good sight.

BRAVE SPARROW: You are still wise, Blind Owl. White Horse and all the villagers say so.

BLIND OWL: At my age, it is all I have left. But if I were truly wise, I would have died at Wounded Knee Creek with the many others. That would have been a wise thing to do. It would have spared me so much misery. One of my sons and three of my granddaughters murdered. I could not see it happen, but I felt it all the same.

GRAY CLOUD: We all have had nothing but misery. But we saw it with our own eyes.

BRAVE SPARROW: *(To GRAY CLOUD.)* Enough, daughter. Say no more.

BLIND OWL: I still can't see what you are doing.

SPOTTED DEER: Sewing beads. My father was able to trade some skins for beads.

BRAVE SPARROW: We're making belts and pouches and jewelry. Gray Cloud is almost as good at it as I am. Spotted Deer is... still learning.

BLIND OWL: Sewing beads! Jewelry! When there is no food!

BRAVE SPARROW: The ground is too frozen to plant. When the sun warms the earth, we can start planting. Until then, we sew beads.

BLIND OWL: Frozen. All of the dead Lakotas froze in the blizzard. When we returned three days later, the White Man had taken all the frozen bodies and thrown them into a big pit. I could not count them with these eyes, but the elders did. They said it was over two hundred, including the women and children. The soldiers then covered the pit with dirt and stone.

BRAVE SPARROW: There was no burial ceremony for my family. For anyone. All we could do was mourn quietly. *(Pause.)*

BLIND OWL: What can you do with beaded goods when we are starving?

SPOTTED DEER: We are going to sell them to the White Man! We can trade for food. Or even the White Man's money!

BRAVE SPARROW: The White Man knows the Lakota beaded wear is very beautiful. They buy them. As fast as we can make them.

BLIND OWL: *(With disgust.)* White Man! What White Man? *(Realizes.)* You mean the soldiers?

SPOTTED DEER: Especially the soldiers. They buy them and send them back to their homes far away.

BLIND OWL: You are selling to the very same men who less than two moons ago slaughtered our tribe at Wounded Knee Creek? The soldiers who killed your two sons and Gray Cloud's husband? The same ones who murdered my eldest son and three of my granddaughters?!

BRAVE SPARROW: These are different soldiers.

BLIND OWL: *(In disbelief.)* Are they?

BRAVE SPARROW: White Horse and the men say all those soldiers were ordered back to the fort at Pine Ridge. They are to stand trial for what they did.

BLIND OWL: Pine Ridge?

SPOTTED DEER: That is where Father is today!

BLIND OWL: White Horse went to Pine Ridge?

BRAVE SPARROW: With three other Lakota men. They have been ordered by the militia to testify. They are to speak and say what they saw on that day.

BLIND OWL: No White Man is going to believe what any Lakota says.

BRAVE SPARROW: The four men were ordered to testify. Perhaps the officers will listen.

GRAY CLOUD: *(Bitter.)* Maybe the soldiers who killed my husband will be punished! He was unarmed. They had already taken his rifle away.

BLIND OWL: Most of the Lakota men were unarmed. And of course, so were the wives and the children. I can still hear the screams in my sleep. *(Weeps.)*

BRAVE SPARROW: The time for weeping is over, Blind Owl. Now we must work to survive.

BLIND OWL: *(With disgust.)* With beads and cloth!

SPOTTED DEER: Mother, is this better? *(Hands her the beaded cloth.)*

BRAVE SPARROW: Much better, little one. Nice and tight. *(Returns it to her.)* Someday you will be as good at beading as your sister.

SPOTTED DEER: *(Delighted.)* I will?

BLIND OWL: I could never do bead work because of my poor sight, but I can feel the beading and tell if it is good or not.

SPOTTED DEER: Will you feel mine, Blind Owl?

BLIND OWL: Are you sure? I am very critical.

SPOTTED DEER: Please?

BLIND OWL: Then I will, little one. *(SPOTTED DEER hands the old woman her beading. BLIND OWL touches it and feels it thoroughly.)* Hmmmmm… *(A long pause.)*

BRAVE SPARROW: Do not tease the girl, Blind Owl! Say what you think.

BLIND OWL: I think… it is too fine a piece for any White Man! *(Laughs.)* You have a gift, little one!

SPOTTED DEER: Thank you, Blind Owl!

BLIND OWL: I wish I could see the colors. When I was very young, I could still see some colors.

SPOTTED DEER: This one is red and yellow with black trim.

BLIND OWL: It sounds very pretty. *(SOUND EFFECT: HORSES APPROACHING.)* I hear horses. Three or four of them.

GRAY CLOUD: *(Frightened.)* Soldiers?

BLIND OWL: No, they are not soldiers' horses.

BRAVE SPARROW: Maybe it is White Horse and the other men! *(Rises.)*

SPOTTED DEER: Father? *(Rises.)* Back from Pine Ridge? *(BRAVE SPARROW and SPOTTED DEER EXIT RIGHT. VOICES are heard OFF RIGHT.)*

GRAY CLOUD: *(Bitter.)* If you are so wise, old lady, tell me what has happened!

BLIND OWL: Nothing good… nothing good. *(WHITE HORSE ENTERS RIGHT in native clothes, but without a blanket to keep him warm. He is followed IN by BRAVE SPARROW and SPOTTED DEER.)*

BRAVE SPARROW: *(To WHITE HORSE.)* Come close to the fire, my husband! *(To GRAY CLOUD.)* Make room for your father, Gray Cloud.

WHITE HORSE: *(Sees BLIND OWL.)* It is Blind Owl, I see. You are welcome here.

BLIND OWL: Come close to the fire, White Horse. I can feel the frozen water on you from here. *(WHITE HORSE squats by the fire and warms his hands.)*

BRAVE SPARROW: I am so glad you are back! I was afraid the soldiers would keep you there all day and night.

GRAY CLOUD: What happened, Father?

WHITE HORSE: They only let us speak a short time each. We told them what we saw, how it started, the whole story.

BLIND OWL: Did they ask you any questions?

WHITE HORSE: None. It seemed they just wanted us to speak and leave.

BRAVE SPARROW: Did they listen to you?

WHITE HORSE: A few did. Most did not.

BLIND OWL: I said no White Man would listen to a Lakota!

BRAVE SPARROW: Then why were you gone so long?

WHITE HORSE: After they ordered us out of the room, Dark Hawk and the others decided to stay in Pine Ridge to hear what the outcome was. So I stayed with them. We had to wait no longer than an hour.

BLIND OWL: And…?

BRAVE SPARROW: What did you hear?

GRAY CLOUD: Will they punish the soldiers who killed my husband?

WHITE HORSE: No. There will be no punishment.

BRAVE SPARROW: None at all?

WHITE HORSE: *(Rises to stand, quietly angry.)* Very much the opposite. The court declared that none of the officers at Wounded Knee Creek were guilty of any misconduct. They told the officers that they acted in the correct manner.

BLIND OWL: Killing over two hundred Lakotas? That is the correct manner for the White Man?

BRAVE SPARROW: *(Goes to WHITE HORSE and embraces him.)* Oh, my husband!

GRAY CLOUD: *(Bitter.)* Then there is no justice.

WHITE HORSE: Right before we mounted to leave, a White Man came out of the court and told everyone that the Secretary of War in Washington is recommending that twenty of the soldiers be awarded the Medal of Honor.

SPOTTED DEER: What is that, Father?

WHITE HORSE: It is a prize they give for bravery in battle.

BLIND OWL: What battle? It was a massacre!

BRAVE SPARROW: *(Weeps.)* No justice! No hope!

GRAY CLOUD: What do we do now, Father?

WHITE HORSE: *(Unsteady.)* We... we...

BLIND OWL: We just wait to die. That is what my so-called wisdom tells me!

WHITE HORSE: No. We wait until the sun warms the earth, and then we plant the seeds. *(LIGHTS SLOWLY FADE OUT.)*

AFTERMATH

The Wounded Knee Massacre has been studied over the years. Based on eyewitness accounts, the incident has been proven to be a massacre and not a battle. In 2001, the National Congress of American Indians passed two resolutions condemning the awarding of Medals of Honor to men who did not act out of bravery but rather through cruelty. A monument was erected at Wounded Knee in remembrance of the Native Americans who died there. Today, the Wounded Knee Battlefield is a U. S. National Historic Landmark.

MUSIC IN THE AIR
(1906)

BACKGROUND

Reginald Fessenden was one of the leading pioneers in the development of radio as we know it today. He was born in Canada to an American father and did most of his scientific work in the United States. Fessenden worked with other scientists to transition from transmitting only Morse Code via radio waves to transmitting spoken words. He made the first two-way transatlantic radio transmission in 1906, and in December of that year, he did experimental broadcasts from a 420-foot radio tower in Brant Rock, Massachusetts. His signals were picked up by radio enthusiasts hundreds of miles away. On Christmas Eve in 1906, Fessenden produced a holiday broadcast that included music. It is believed to be the first time music was ever broadcast over the radio.

SETTING

TIME: December 24, 1906.
PLACE: A small radio broadcast studio in Brant Rock, Massachusetts.

CHARACTERS

REGINALD FESSENDEN (M)..... inventor
MISS BENT (F).............................. his assistant
HARRIGAN (M)........................... technician
HELEN FESSENDEN (F) .... Fessenden's wife

SET DESCRIPTION

The studio is a shed built at the base of a radio tower. The room is crowded with large and bulky radio transmitting equipment. There is a desk UP LEFT on which sits a stack of papers and a primitive microphone. Two chairs sit at the desk. A table with a gramophone on it sits RIGHT. There is a record on the gramophone and an additional record next to it. The shed has one window and one door RIGHT.

PROPERTIES

Pocket watch (REGINALD); kettle and cups on a tray (HELEN); roll of twine (HARRIGAN).

SOUND EFFECTS AND MUSIC

Curious radio noises, recordings of "O Holy Night" and George Fredric Handel's "Largo."

FLEXIBLE CASTING NOTE

MISS BENT could be played as MR. BENT with only minor script adjustments.

LIGHTS UP on REGINALD FESSENDEN and MISS BENT, looking over papers at the desk. He is dressed in a period suit, and she is in a long dark dress with a white blouse and warm jacket. It is 8:52 in the evening.

REGINALD: These look fine, Miss Bent. And did you type out the Bible quotation for tonight?

BENT: Yes, Mr. Fessenden. It's here somewhere. *(Looks through the papers.)*

REGINALD: Did you type it in all upper case letters, as I asked?

BENT: Oh, yes. *(Finds the paper.)* Here it is. Two copies, like you said. *(Hands them to him.)*

REGINALD: I think it will be easier for you and my wife to read it this way. *(Looks at the sheets.)* This is fine.

BENT: I feel I should tell you, Mr. Fessenden, that I am very nervous about this.

REGINALD: No reason to be. You'll be reading with Helen. Like a small chorus.

BENT: All the same— *(HARRIGAN ENTERS RIGHT, wearing a heavy coat over his work pants and flannel shirt. He carries a roll of twine.)*

REGINALD: Harrigan! How's the weather holding out?

HARRIAGAN: It's starting to snow.

BENT: Oh, dear…

HARRIGAN: *(To BENT.)* Just flurries. *(To REGINALD.)* I'm more concerned about the wind. It's kicking up a bit, and some of the wire cables are flapping away. I got some twine from the barn. I better tie some of the cable to the tower poles to keep it steady. We don't want the wire snapping loose during the transmission.

REGINALD: Excellent idea, Harrigan.

HARRIGAN: Have we got enough time?

REGINALD: *(Looks at his pocket watch.)* Just 'bout.

HARRIGAN: Then I better get to it. *(Heads to the door.)*

BENT: Be careful up there, Mr. Harrigan! If it's so windy—

HARRIGAN: *(Smiles at her.)* Don't concern yourself, Miss Bent. I'll be all right. *(EXITS RIGHT.)*

REGINALD: Harrigan knows that tower well. All 420 feet of it. He practically built the thing all by himself.

BENT: It's just that it's so high!

REGINALD: Is the gramophone all cranked up, Miss Bent? And have you put the records in the right order?

BENT: I think so. *(Crosses to the gramophone.)* First, "O Holy Night", and then, Handel's "Largo"— *(The door blows open, and HELEN FESSENDEN ENTERS RIGHT, carrying a tray with a kettle and cups on it. She wears a heavy coat and hat that have some snow on them.)*

REGINALD: Helen! About time. What have you got there?

HELEN: Someone close this door behind me! My hands are full! *(BENT closes the door.)* I thought some hot cocoa might be useful. You really need to get a stove in this shack.

BENT: How thoughtful of you, Mrs. Fessenden. *(HELEN puts the tray on the desk.)* We should drink it while it's hot.

REGINALD: Not near the microphone! And all those wires! If it should spill—!

BENT: *(Takes the tray.)* I'll put it over here on the table. *(Sets the tray on the table.)* No wires over here.

REGINALD: Not too close to the gramophone.

HELEN: Reggie, what is Mr. Harrigan doing climbing that tower like a monkey in a tree?

REGINALD: He is securing some of the wire cable.

HELEN: Well, I hope he doesn't blow away. It's quite windy out there. And there's a little snow, too. *(Pours the cocoa into the cups.)* Come and drink up, everyone.

REGINALD: Helen, I'm not sure we have time. I don't want to start the transmission late. I plan on nine o'clock sharp.

HELEN: How can it be late? *(Gives cups to BENT and REGINALD.)* No one knows you're going to broadcast tonight. You're just sending those radio waves out hoping someone is listening.

REGINALD: That's why I chose nine o'clock. Most radio enthusiasts are listening for signals in the evening.

BENT: *(Sips her cocoa.)* This is delicious, Mrs. Fessenden!

HELEN: Thank you, Miss Bent. *(Sips her cocoa.)*

REGINALD: They have sold thousands of crystal sets during the past year. There could be a lot of people listening. Why, I'll bet in New York City alone, there are over one hundred radio listeners tonight.

HELEN: New York! You don't imagine your radio waves will travel that far away!

REGINALD: It is very likely. With the new tower—

HELEN: Drink your cocoa, Reggie. Now, what happens if one—or a bunch—of these listeners tries to radio back to you?

REGINALD: They can't. We're on a frequency that sends out messages but doesn't receive any back.

HELEN: That's like having a telephone where you can talk to someone but they can't talk back to you.

BENT: That's why it's called a broadcast, Mrs. Fessenden. You send out radio waves broadly in all directions. It's just for listening.

REGINALD: *(Testy.)* Don't waste your time trying to explain these things to my wife, Miss Bent.

HELEN: *(Miffed.)* I like that! I understand more than you think. Now, what's this about sending out music?

REGINALD: That was Miss Bent's idea, really!

BENT: *(Shy.)* Not really. I just said—

REGINALD: I asked Miss Bent what she would most like to hear on a Christmas Eve broadcast and—

BENT: And I said Christmas hymns.

REGINALD: A brilliant idea! I don't think it's ever been done before!

HELEN: *(To REGINALD.)* Can you actually send out music on these radio waves of yours? I mean… they're not actually words. Won't it all come out like dribble?

REGINALD: Helen, we are sending out sounds, not words. Why, you could broadcast a dog barking, and it could be heard for what it is.

HELEN: A dog! Honestly, Reggie!

REGINALD: *(Looks at his pocket watch.)* We've got just enough time for you two to practice the Bible verse. *(Hands the sheets to HELEN and BENT.)* Come over here to the microphone and speak right into it.

HELEN: Reggie, I'm not so sure about this! I am not an actress!

BENT: Neither am I.

REGINALD: You'll both be fine. I've heard you read the psalms in church, Helen. It's the same thing.

HELEN: I wasn't reading for a bunch of radio nuts in New York City!

REGINALD: Now I'll give you the signal so you both start reading at the same time. *(Points.)* Just like this. Ready… set… *(Points.)*

HELEN/BENT: *(Read.)* "Glory to God in the highest, and on Earth, peace to men of good will!"

REGINALD: That's pretty good. But not so fast. If there's static in the transmission, the listeners will miss a whole word or two.

BENT: I am so nervous, Mrs. Fessenden!

HELEN: I've got some butterflies in my stomach, too! *(HARRIGAN ENTERS RIGHT, shaking off the snow on him.)*

REGINALD: Are we set to go, Harrigan?

HARRIGAN: All set, I think. *(Goes to the radio equipment and starts turning dials and switches. SOUND EFFECT: CURIOUS RADIO NOISES.)* Just give her a chance to warm up.

REGINALD: *(Looks at his pocket watch.)* Only a few minutes late. Harrigan, signal us when the microphone is live.

HELEN: Live?

BENT: That means it's turned on.

REGINALD: And once it is on, no talking or other noises.

HELEN: Mr. Harrigan, would you like a cup of hot cocoa?

REGINALD: *(Nervous.)* Not now, Helen!

HELEN: But he must be so cold after climbing that tall tower—

HARRIGAN: Five seconds, Mr. Fessenden. Four… Three… *(Mouths "Two… One…")*

REGINALD: *(Speaks into the microphone, very clear and distinct.)* Attention! Attention to all who can hear my voice! I am Reginald Fessenden transmitting from Brant Rock, Massachusetts, on this Christmas Eve, and we wish all out there our warmest holiday greetings! Do not try to respond to this transmission, as it is not a person-to-person radio message. Instead, it is what we call a broadcast. We are sending out a brief, but hopefully enlightening, Christmas Eve message to all. And our message appropriately begins with a short quotation from the Bible that I am sure you will recognize and appreciate. Here it is… *(Beckons to the HELEN and BENT, and they nervously move up to the microphone. He points, but they both freeze up and cannot speak. REGINALD silently encourages them, but BENT gets dizzy and starts to fall over. HELEN helps her to a chair. REGINALD continues on, but the strain is evident.)* Yes, it is a wonderful passage from the New Testament… *(Motions to HELEN for a copy of the sheet, and she quickly hands it to him.)* …and it goes like this… *(Reads, more relaxed.)* "Glory to God in the highest, and on Earth, peace to men of good will!" Better and truer words have never been spoken on a Christmas Eve. *(Takes the microphone to the gramophone where BENT has recovered enough to turn on the switch and hold the* *armature in position.)* And now for something very special as part of our broadcast. We are going to play some appropriate music for this special occasion. That is correct, listeners, I said music. We will now hear the lovely sound of that beloved Christmas hymn, "O Holy Night." *(Signals to BENT, who carefully drops the needle, and SOUND EFFECT: "O Holy Night" PLAYS. While the record plays, there is pantomimed dialogue between REGINALD, BENT, and HELEN. BENT profusely apologizes to REGINALD for fainting, who nods understanding. HELEN comforts her, sitting her down to calm her. REGINALD crosses to HARRIGAN and they whisper quietly, HARRIGAN nodding his head that all is going well. When the record comes to an end, BENT rushes to the gramophone and changes to the next record. REGINALD again takes the microphone.)* In case you have just started picking up our signal, you are listening to Reginald Fessenden transmitting from Brant Rock, Massachusetts, on this Christmas Eve. You have just heard the holiday hymn "O Holy Night" broadcast over the airwaves. We believe it is probably the first time that music has been sent out on radio waves. We hope you enjoyed it. We have another musical treat for you tonight, but before we play it for you, I would like all of you out there listening to consider sending me a postcard or a letter saying where you live and if you heard and enjoyed our Christmas Eve broadcast. Just mail your comments to Reginald Fessenden in Brant Rock, Massachusetts. And now for another musical favorite this time of the year, George Fredric Handel's "Largo." *(Signals BENT to start the record, which she does. SOUND EFFECT: "Largo" PLAYS, and they all stand still listening to it. After a moment, HELEN goes over to REGINALD and embraces him proudly. The LIGHTS and MUSIC FADE OUT.)*

AFTERMATH

Fessenden received many letters from listeners, some as far away as Virginia. He continued to experiment with ways to perfect radio transmission and had hundreds of patents on radio equipment before he died at the age of sixty-five in 1932. By that year, radio was fully established as an entertainment media, and nationwide broadcasting was available to the thousands who bought radios.

THE LETTER E
(1909)

BACKGROUND

Ellis Island, located in the bay of New York City, processed about twelve million immigrants between the years 1892 and 1954. The multi-building complex includes the Great Hall, where foreigners wishing to enter the United States were identified and questioned by authorities. All of the arrivals had to walk up a long staircase, giving officials an opportunity to observe any physical defects, particularly heart problems and signs of consumption (tuberculosis). Every immigrant was also given a medical exam by doctors and nurses, and those with serious ailments were sent to the Ellis Island Immigration Hospital. The island also had dormitories for those detained for further questioning, and there were quarters for those deemed dangerous, mentally deficient, or contagious to ready them for deportation.

SETTING

TIME: March 1909.
PLACE: A waiting room in the immigration building on Ellis Island.

CHARACTERS

NURSE (F) .... American nurse
AVRAM (M) .... Lithuanian immigrant
HASKELL (M).............................. his fifteen-year-old son
BELA (F) .... Avram's wife
JUDITH (F) .... Avram's twelve-year-old daughter
MICHAELA (F) .... Judith's twin

SET DESCRIPTION

The small room consists of a door LEFT, a window RIGHT, and a couple of benches along the UPSTAGE wall. The feeling is that of a jail cell except for the bright light that comes through the unbarred window.

PROPERTIES

Two luggage bundles (HASKELL, AVRAM, BELA, MICHAELA, JUDITH).

FLEXIBLE CASTING NOTE

HASKELL, JUDITH, and MICHAELA could be played by either gender with only minor script adjustments.

LIGHTS UP on the empty, small waiting room. NURSE ENTERS LEFT, followed by HASKELL, AVRAM, BELA, MICHAELA, and JUDITH. The NURSE wears a period nurse's uniform. The FAMILY is dressed in heavy outdoor period clothing, and each carries two bundles of luggage. ALL are frightened, nervous, and wary. The capital letter E is written on HASKELL'S coat in chalk.

NURSE: Come this way, please.

AVRAM: *(To HASKELL.)* What is she saying, Haskell?

HASKELL: We are to follow her, Papa.

BELA: What is this place?

NURSE: You are to wait here until the doctor is ready for you.

HASKELL: Doctor? *(NURSE EXITS LEFT, closing the door behind her.)*

AVRAM: We should follow her?

HASKELL: No, Papa. She said to wait in here. *(They put their bundles on the floor.)*

BELA: That is not all she said. Tell us, Haskell.

HASKELL: Something about a doctor. I didn't understand it all.

BELA: A doctor?

AVRAM: But we were all already examined by a doctor! We are not ill!

HASKELL: I do not know enough English words yet, Papa. I cannot understand everything that they are saying to us.

BELA: Two weeks in the bottom of a ship! It is a miracle that we are not all sick.

JUDITH: Michaela was seasick!

MICHAELA: Only the first two days.

JUDITH: I didn't get seasick. I am a good sailor.

AVRAM: Haskell, do you know enough English to tell me what that word is they put on your coat? *(Points to the E.)*

HASKELL: It is not a word, Papa. It is just a letter of the alphabet. The letter E.

BELA: What does it mean, son? You can tell us.

HASKELL: It can mean anything. Any word that starts with the letter E. The English word for elephant starts with the letter E.

AVRAM: I do not think a doctor put that on your coat because he thinks you are an elephant! *(MICHAELA and JUDITH laugh.)*

BELA: Judith! Michaela! Shush! This is a serious matter.

HASKELL: I just used the word elephant as an example.

AVRAM: Why would you know the English word for elephant? What use is that to us?

JUDITH: Mama, are there elephants in America?

MICHAELA: Or tigers?

BELA: Shush!

HASKELL: The letter E can be for many words. It could be for eagle or—

AVRAM: More animals!

HASKELL: One of the English books I found was about going to the zoo.

AVRAM: What is a zoo?

HASKELL: I... *(Defeated.)* I don't know. Something to do with animals.

BELA: Why did they put that chalk mark on you and not the rest of us?

HASKELL: I cannot say, Mama. I saw other English letters put on other people.

BELA: This is a crazy place! Why are we put in this jail cell?

JUDITH: It's not a jail, Mama.

MICHAELA: *(Opens the door a little.)* The door is not locked.

BELA: They're making me feel like a criminal!

AVRAM: Bela, calm yourself. *(Takes her to the window.)* Come and look out the window. You can see across the water to the city. That is where we are going soon!

BELA: *(Annoyed.)* I can see, I can see! I have eyes!

HASKELL: *(To himself.)* Eyes...

AVRAM: What's that you are saying, Haskell?

HASKELL: Nothing, Papa. *(The door OPENS, and NURSE ENTERS LEFT.)*

NURSE: *(To HASKELL.)* The doctor can see you now. Come along. *(Beckons for HASKELL to follow.)*

AVRAM: *(To HASKELL.)* What is she saying, Haskell?

HASKELL: *(To AVRAM and BELA.)* I am to go with her and see a doctor.

BELA: Why? Ask her why!

HASKELL: *(To NURSE, timid.)* Madame Nurse... why doctor?

NURSE: *(Looks at the letter E on his coat.)* E. He wants to check your eyes. Come along.

AVRAM: What does she say, Haskell?

HASKELL: *(To AVRAM and BELA.)* The doctor wants to look at my eyes.

NURSE: This way. *(HASKELL and NURSE EXIT LEFT.)*

BELA: His eyes! There is nothing the matter with his eyes!

MICHAELA: But didn't you notice, Mama?

JUDITH: Haskell's eyes are all red.

MICHAELA: And he told us that they itch.

BELA: Shush!

AVRAM: I noticed it as well, Bela. The past few days, the boy's eyes have been red.

BELA: It is nothing! It comes from looking at those books with the English words!

MICHAELA: Papa, will they let Haskell into America if he has red eyes?

BELA: Of course they will! It is nothing serious.

AVRAM: Bela, we were told. From the very beginning. They will not take anyone who has a disease or—

BELA: *(Angry.)* Haskell has no disease!

AVRAM: We must be prepared for the worse.

BELA: *(Desperate.)* Do not say such things, Avram! Please!

MICHAELA: If Haskell cannot go to America, then I don't want to go!

JUDITH: Me, neither! I will get back on the ship! I am a good sailor!

BELA: *(To JUDITH and MICHAELA.)* Stop talking nonsense, you two!

AVRAM: I am told there is a hospital on this island. Perhaps they will put Haskell there until he is well again.

BELA: *(Furious.)* Hospital! My son is already well! *(To JUDITH and MICHAELA.)* And no more talk about going back! We will never go back to Lithuania! America is our home now!

AVRAM: *(To JUDITH and MICHAELA.)* Your mama is right. This is our home now.

MICHAELA: *(Tearful.)* But without Haskell?

JUDITH: His eyes are not too red. Only a little.

MICHAELA: And I think they were already getting better.

AVRAM: All we can do is wait here and pray to God that Haskell can join us.

BELA: I will not leave this island without my dear son! *(The door OPENS, and ALL turn fearfully as NURSE ENTERS LEFT.)*

NURSE: Gather your things.

BELA: *(To AVRAM.)* What is she saying?

AVRAM: I do not know...

NURSE: Gather your things! *(Picks up one of the bundles and hands it to JUDITH.)* Time to go. *(HASKELL APPEARS in the doorway.)*

BELA: Haskell! *(Rushes to him and embraces him.)*

HASKELL: Everything is all right, Mama. *(Holds out his palm for all to see.)* Look!

MICHAELA: What is it?

HASKEL: Cinders! They must have blown out of the ship's smoke stack. The doctor found them in my eyes!

AVRAM: No wonder they were red!

HASKELL: He used this wooden stick thing and was able to get them out of my eyes. It hurt a little. But now they are gone, and my eyes don't itch!

BELA: My Haskell is well?

HASKELL: Very well, Mama. *(Embraces her again.)*

NURSE: Time to gather your things and get to the dock if you want to catch the next boat to the Battery. *(EXITS LEFT.)*

AVRAM: What did she say?

HASKELL: Something about a boat. We are free to go down to the dock. That is where we will get the boat to the city.

MICHAELA: Then you're coming with us, Haskell?

HASKELL: *(Laughs.)* Of course I am! You did not think I'd let you go to America without me!

AVRAM: Girls, get your things! We must not waste time. There is a boat we have to catch. *(ALL gather up their bundles.)*

BELA: Another boat! I hope the water is not too rough.

JUDITH: I don't mind. I am a good sailor!

AVRAM: Come along, little sailor! You, too, Michaela. I will lead the way. *(EXITS LEFT, followed by JUDITH and MICHAELA.)*

BELA: *(Embraces HASKELL again.)* My son! I was so worried!

HASKELL: Nothing to worry about now, Mama. We are going to America!

BELA: I was afraid they would not let you come with us.

HASKELL: *(Points to the E on his coat.)* You see this, Mama?

BELA: Yes...

HASKELL: It is an E. That stands for eyes. So I am not an elephant after all! *(Laughs.)*

AVRAM: *(ENTERS LEFT.)* Come, both of you! You don't want to be late for America, do you? *(EXITS LEFT, followed by BELA and HASKELL. LIGHTS FADE OUT.)*

AFTERMATH

After immigration processing ceased on Ellis Island in 1954, the whole island was abandoned, and it deteriorated until 1965 when the site was listed on the National Register of Historic Places. Restoring the main buildings cost $150 million, and in 1990 the island was opened to the public as a museum. Today, Ellis Island receives about two million visitors each year. It has been estimated that approximately forty percent of all current citizens of the United States can trace at least one of their ancestors to Ellis Island.

CAUGHT IN THE WIRE
(1918)

BACKGROUND

During World War I, a deadly influenza epidemic arose in Europe, but England, France, and Germany kept the news of the epidemic out of the newspapers. In neutral Spain, however, cases of the epidemic were made public, and the new strain was subsequently called the Spanish Flu by the rest of the world. The first cases of the epidemic in the United States were found at a military hospital in Kansas in March of 1918. Within four months, the epidemic had spread across the country. In Philadelphia, 4,597 people died in one week. Unlike most forms of influenza, the Spanish Flu affected all ages, from healthy young children to the very elderly. But those in poor health, particularly wounded soldiers from the war, were the most susceptible.

SETTING

TIME: November 1918.

PLACE: Mrs. Carter's rooming house in Philadelphia.

CHARACTERS

FRANKLIN (M) .... young soldier returned from Europe

MRS. CARTER (F) .... Franklin's widowed mother

CHARLENE (F) .... Franklin's twelve-year-old sister

MRS. LANSKY (F) .... aging midwife

SET DESCRIPTION

The room is simply furnished with a bed LEFT. Two chairs sit next to the bed. A nightstand and dresser line the walls. A door is RIGHT.

PROPERTIES

Bucket of water, small towel (MRS. CARTER); bucket of water (CHARLENE); socks (FRANKLIN).

LIGHTS UP on FRANKLIN, lying in bed in a nightshirt covered by blankets. He is mostly unconscious, but occasionally coughs and mumbles. MRS. CARTER sits in a chair by the bed and puts a cold, wet towel on his forehead, pulling it from a bucket of water at her side. She wears a full-length work dress with an apron and has her hair in a tight bun.

FRANKLIN: *(In a feverish nightmare.)* Over the top, men! In twenty seconds... over the top!

MRS. CARTER: It's all right, Franklin! You're home now. Safe and sound.

FRANKLIN: You hear that, men? Twenty seconds... over the top!

MRS. CARTER: It's Mama talking to you, Franklin! You're home!

FRANKLIN: Twenty seconds... and then you die! Fifteen seconds left!

MRS. CARTER: You're home in your own bed in your own home in Philadelphia!

FRANKLIN: Over the top, men... and in ten seconds, you die!

MRS. CARTER: *(Desperate.)* Stop it, Franklin! Please!

FRANKLIN: *(Wakes up.)* Mama?

MRS. CARTER: I'm here, Franklin!

FRANKLIN: *(Confused.)* Mama?

MRS. CARTER: Right here.

FRANKLIN: It's so hot... I feel so hot...

MRS. CARTER: It's the fever. Let me help cool you off.

FRANKLIN: I... I... *(Falls asleep. MRS. CARTER puts the wet towel back on his forehead. CHARLENE ENTERS RIGHT, tentatively. She wears a worn dress, coat, and laced-up shoes.)*

MRS. CARTER: Charlene! When's Doc Bordman coming?

CHARLENE: He wasn't at his office, Mama. Mrs. Bordman said he was at the hospital.

MRS. CARTER: Which hospital? We got to get him here quick!

CHARLENE: St. Luke's.

MRS. CATER: Then hurry, child! Go find him!

CHARLENE: I already been there. They said all the doctors were too busy to see anyone.

MRS. CARTER: What?!

CHARLENE: Mama, they got all kind of sick people there. In the halls and everywhere. 'Cause of the... the pan... demic.

MRS. CARTER: The what? Talk sense, Charlene!

CHARLENE: The man says it's a... pandemic. This Spanish Flu thing. It's what killed Mrs. Gordon next door. And Little Henry down the block. Last week, three girls in my class came down with it. I'll bet they're all dead, too.

MRS. CARTER: But your brother needs a doctor! What are we going to do?

CHARLENE: I seen Mrs. Lansky come in downstairs just a minute ago. She said she's here to look after one of the boarders.

MRS. CARTER: One of *my* boarders? Who?

CHARLENE: Mr. Wilcox up on the third floor. Mrs. Lansky says she was sent for by Mrs. Wilcox. She thinks he's got the Spanish Flu.

MRS. CARTER: The Spanish Flu! In my boarding house!

CHARLENE: That's why Mrs. Lansky come to look at him.

MRS. CARTER: But Mrs. Lansky is just a midwife! What can she know of influenza?

CHARLENE: They say she's almost as good as a nurse. Everybody is callin' on her.

MRS. CARTER: Franklin's just got a little fever, that's all. But he needs a doctor.

CHARLENE: You want me to go up and ask Mrs. Lansky to come and look at Franklin, her bein' in the house already?

MRS. CARTER: No! Oh, dear God, help us! Charlene, you bring up another bucket of cold water.

CHARLENE: Yes, Mama. *(Starts to leave.)*

MRS. CARTER: Make it as cold as you can.

CHARLENE: Yes, Mama.

MRS. CARTER: Wait! I think... Maybe you better go upstairs first and ask Mrs. Lansky if she'd be so kind as to come and look at my Franklin.

CHARLENE: Yes, Mama. *(EXITS RIGHT. MRS. CARTER removes the wet towel and puts it back in the bucket.)*

FRANKLIN: *(Stirs again.)* Watch out for the wire! It's everywhere, men! Don't get caught in the wire!

MRS. CARTER: There's no more wire, dear. It's all far, far away. You're home now, son.

FRANKLIN: Gotta help Owens! He's caught in the wire!

MRS. CARTER: It's your Mama, son. Don't you hear me?

FRANKLIN: *(Opens his eyes.)* Mama?

MRS. CARTER: I'm right here, Franklin!

FRANKLIN: How come it's so hot? Is it summer already?

MRS. CARTER: No, son. It's November. It's just that you got a little fever, that's all.

FRANKLIN: Some of them in the trenches got the fever.

MRS. CARTER: Well, you're not in the trenches any more, Franklin. You're home safe and sound.

FRANKLIN: Was I having another fit, Mama? Was I crazy again? Like before?

MRS. CARTER: It's just the fever, son. It gives you bad dreams.

FRANKLIN: It seems like all I have since I come home is bad dreams. Day and night. Even when I'm awake.

MRS. CARTER: That will all go away once this little fever breaks. I promise you.

FRANKLIN: It's the gas! Ever since that chlorine came creeping over the hill—

MRS. CARTER: Hush, Franklin! Don't talk about it again. You know how it upsets you.

FRANKLIN: They ran out of gas masks, and there it was coming over the hill!

MRS. CARTER: *(Panics.)* Franklin! Stop! *(Pause.)*

FRANKLIN: Better get some sleep… Been up for twenty hours… Sleep, men. Get some sleep while you can… *(Falls asleep.)*

MRS. CARTER: Oh, dear God, help my son. *(Quietly prays. MRS. LANSKY APPEARS in the doorway. She wears a heavy coat and hat.)*

MRS. LANSKY: Mrs. Carter?

MRS. CARTER: Oh, Mrs. Lansky. *(Crosses to her.)* So kind of you to come. How is Mr. Wilcox?

MRS. LANSKY: Spanish Flu. One of the worst cases I seen.

MRS. CARTER: Mr. Wilcox? But he's as strong a man I seen, working construction and all.

MRS. LANSKY: This kind of influenza don't care about age or health or anything. In all my years, I never come across anything like it. All the hospitals are full, not that there is much they can do there. Just hope and pray that it passes.

MRS. CARTER: But some do recover, don't they?

MRS. LANSKY: Oh, yes. But there's no rhyme or reason for who survives and who doesn't. I don't think Mr. Wilcox will make it 'til morning.

MRS. CARTER: Oh, God help him!

MRS. LANSKY: Your daughter said your boy is sick?

MRS. CARTER: Yes. We tried to get Doc Bordman, but—

MRS. LANSKY: But you ended up calling on me. I understand and I don't take offense. I'm no doctor, but I seen all kinds of sickness in my sixty-eight years. Can I take a look at him?

MRS. CARTER: He's sleeping right now.

MRS. LANSKY: It don't matter. *(Crosses to the bed.)* Your daughter says he's got a fever.

MRS. CARTER: Yes. But he pulled through influenza when he was only twelve and was strong as an ox afterwards.

MRS. LANSKY: That was no Spanish Flu. *(Touches FRANKLIN'S forehead.)*

MRS. CARTER: His name's Franklin. Just like his late father. Franklin's just come home from France two months ago. From the war, you see—

MRS. LANSKY: Was he sick then?

MRS. CARTER: No! I mean, not physically. But he was gassed in France, and Doc Bordman said he was suffering from something called shell shock and—

MRS. LANSKY: I seen plenty of that this past year. *(Pulls up each of FRANKLIN'S eyelids and examines his eyes.)*

MRS. CARTER: *(Alarmed.)* What are you doing?

MRS. LANSKY: *(Crosses to the foot of the bed.)* I need to feel his feet. Help me get his socks off.

MRS. CARTER: His feet? *(Helps MRS. LANSKY pull up the covers and remove FRANKLIN'S socks.)* I don't understand.

MRS. LANSKY: You been dousing his forehead with water, I suppose?

MRS. CARTER: Yes. Shouldn't I have?

MRS. LANSKY: Don't make much difference. But with that wet forehead so cool, I gotta go by his feet. *(Holds one foot in her hands, and then another. A long pause. She puts his feet down and covers them back up.)* Now I gotta feel his neck. *(Places her hands on either side of his neck.)* Swollen glands. Not so much as some, but still swollen.

MRS. CARTER: What are you saying?

MRS. LANSKY: I'm sorry, Mrs. Carter. It's the Spanish Flu, all right. Of course he might pull through. But these boys coming back from France are in pretty bad shape to begin with. Most don't make it through this epidemic. But some do.

MRS. CARTER: Oh, dear God! *(Collapses into a chair.)* It's all my fault!

MRS. LANSKY: Spanish Flu is nobody's fault.

MRS. CARTER: You don't understand me. Oh, I am an evil woman, Mrs. Lansky!

MRS. LANSKY: Don't let your grief make you imagine things, Mrs. Carter.

MRS. CARTER: I can tell you. Maybe you can understand. Ever since Franklin came home, he has been in a living hell. Nightmares! Thinks he's seeing things! Shouting out in his sleep. And when he's awake, too. Doc Bordman says he may never get over what he saw and done in France. And when Franklin was in a real bad way, I prayed to God to put him out of his misery. And now you say he has this terrible influenza and might die and it's all my fault! *(Weeps.)*

MRS. LANSKY: You are not an evil woman, Mrs. Carter. You are a mother. And you are not alone. Thousands of mothers are feeling the same kind of guilt about thousands of sons. You take care of your Franklin the best you can and let God decide what happens.

MRS. CARTER: You are being too kind. I don't deserve it.

MRS. LANSKY: Nonsense.

MRS. CARTER: I don't know how to thank you—

CHARLENE: *(ENTERS RIGHT, carrying a bucket of cold water.)* I got it as cold as I could, Mama!

MRS. LANSKY: That's a good girl. That will help keep your brother nice and cool.

CHARLENE: Mrs. Lansky, is Franklin going to be all right?

MRS. LANSKY: Too early to say, my dear. Do you know where Freida Patterson lives?

CHARLENE: Sure do! She's in my class. The Pattersons live on the corner, right above the bakery.

MRS. LANSKY: Thank you.

CHARLENE: I can show you! Just come with me, and we'll be there in no time— *(Rushes OFF RIGHT.)*

MRS. CARTER: Little Freida Patterson?

MRS. LANSKY: They think it's the Spanish Flu. I better get on over there.

MRS. CARTER: Thank you, Mrs. Lansky.

MRS. LANSKY: You tend to your boy as best you can. Cold wet towels are good, but don't let the sheets get wet. *(Starts to leave.)* Oh, and another suggestion.

MRS. CARTER: Yes?

MRS. LANSKY: Your daughter...

MRS. CARTER: Charlene?

MRS. LANSKY: Yes, Charlene. Keep her away from school. It's too dangerous. And keep her away from Franklin, too.

CHARLENE: *(From OFF RIGHT.)* This way, Mrs. Lansky! *(MRS. LANSKY EXITS RIGHT.)*

FRANKLIN: *(Shouts out in his fever.)* Over the top, men... and in ten seconds, you die!

AFTERMATH

Before the epidemic ceased in December of 1920, approximately seventy-five million people worldwide had died of the Spanish Flu. In America, where between 500,000 to 675,000 people perished, the life expectancy for the nation dropped twelve percent. Scientists and doctors still disagree exactly what started the epidemic and why it ceased after two years, but it was the most deadly pandemic of modern times, killing more people than the Black Death in the Middle Ages.

TINY PIECES OF LIGHT
(1920)

BACKGROUND

Philo T. Farnsworth was born in 1906 in a log cabin in rural Utah. As a young boy, he became fascinated with electricity when his family moved to a house in Rigby that had electricity run by a generator. While still young, he experimented with electricity, worked on old motors and discarded generators, and even electrified his mother's washing tub. By the time he got to high school, Philo had already invented a few playful gadgets that ran on electricity and won a science magazine contest with his invention of a magnetized car door lock.

SETTING

TIME: 4:30 p.m. on a Tuesday in October 1920.

PLACE: The science classroom at Rigby High School in Rigby, Utah.

CHARACTERS

MISS PENNECOTT (F) .... high school English teacher
PHILO FARNSWORTH (M) .... fifteen-year-old high school student
JUSTIN TOLMAN (M) .... high school science teacher
AGNES FARNSWORTH (F) .... Philo's younger sister in junior high

SET DESCRIPTION

On a CENTER table are various science instruments of the time, including a microscope, Bunsen burner, test tubes, a small electric motor, wires, and various other electrical equipment. There are also sheets of paper with diagrams and charts, along with a pencil. A stool is next to the table, and a periodic chart of the elements hangs on the wall behind it. TOLMAN'S office is OFF RIGHT, and the rest of the school OFF LEFT.

PHILO sits on the stool at the table. He wears trousers, a white shirt, and a sweater vest. Absorbed in his work, he tests frequencies with the motor, writes down figures, then tests again. He repeats this a few times. MISS PENNECOTT ENTERS LEFT wearing a severe gray dress and glasses. Her hair is in a bun, and she looks much older than she is.

PENNECOTT: *(Surprised and upset.)* Philo Farnsworth! What do you think you are doing here at this hour?!

PHILO: Miss Pennecott! Um... Working on a science project.

PENNECOTT: This late in the afternoon? No one's allowed in the science classroom without permission from—

PHILO: Mr. Tolman said I could. He was just here.

PENNECOTT: A likely story, young man. There are dangerous... things in this classroom. No student should be unaccompanied by a member of the faculty!

PHILO: But Miss Pennecott, Mr. Tolman said—

PENNECOTT: Look at all those wires and... such! Who knows what terrible accident could happen?!

PHILO: It's just a twenty-volt battery generator with only—

PENNECOTT: If you devoted half the time you spend on these gadgets to your English compositions, maybe you would be doing better than a grade of C. I just read your homework assignment, and it is... sadly lacking!

TOLMAN: *(ENTERS RIGHT, wearing a period suit and bow tie.)* What seems to be the problem, Miss Pennecott?

PENNECOTT: Mr. Tolman! What are you doing here so late?

TOLMAN: Probably the same thing you are.

PENNECOTT: I was correcting papers in my office.

TOLMAN: So am I. I just came in to see how Philo was getting on.

PENNECOTT: You knew he was in here alone?

TOLMAN: I told him he could work on his science project as long as I was next door.

PENNECOTT: A lot of good being next door will be when he blows up the school with all these dangerous... gizmos!

PHILO: It's just a twenty-volt battery generator with only—

TOLMAN: All quite safe, I assure you, Miss Pennecott.

PENNECOTT: Well... I'm afraid I'll have to take you on your word of honor, Justin Tolman. I am an English composition teacher and not well versed in all this... modern science.

TOLMAN: That's fine, then. Thank you, Miss Pennecott.

PENNECOTT: You're welcome, I'm sure. *(EXITS LEFT, abruptly.)*

PHILO: Gosh! I don't think Miss Pennecott likes me much.

TOLMAN: I don't think Miss Pennecott likes science much. So what have you been up to, Philo? You haven't shown me anything in a few days.

PHILO: It's sort of a new idea... I think. I'm not sure.

TOLMAN: A new electronic gizmo to frighten Miss Pennecott? *(They both laugh.)*

PHILO: So far, it's just on paper. *(Shuffles some of the papers and hands one to TOLMAN.)* It has to do with using electricity to transmit an image.

TOLMAN: You mean light?

PHILO: More than light. Lines really.

TOLMAN: Lines? *(Looks at one of the diagrams.)* I think I see what you mean. Very interesting.

PHILO: Oh, maybe it's already been done. I haven't seen it in any of my science magazines. You would know best.

TOLMAN: This doesn't look at all familiar to me. Where did you come up with this? These lines?

PHILO: You know how when you plow a field for planting?

TOLMAN: *(Laughs.)* Not from first-hand experience!

PHILO: Well, you plow it in rows. Parallel rows. Either straight or curved. And if you look at it, it's just a series of lines.

TOLMAN: Okay...

PHILO: But let's say you are far away, a half mile or so, and you look at a hill that's been plowed. You don't see rows. It all blends together in your eyes. Instead of plowed lines, you see an image, or a shape, or even a figure.

TOLMAN: Eye retention. Of course.

PHILO: *(Picks up a different diagram and shows it to TOLMAN.)* Now, what if you could use electricity to make these lines? Not just make them, but project them?

TOLMAN: Like on a movie screen?

PHILO: Not really. The images would be *in* the screen, not just projected onto it.

TOLMAN: Very intriguing, Philo. *(Picks up another diagram.)* This here looks like a light bulb.

PHILO: It's a glass vacuum tube. It uses light like a light bulb but instead of illuminating, it creates images... all made up of hundreds and hundreds of lines.

TOLMAN: How do the images get inside the glass tube?

PHILO: Electricity!

TOLMAN: By wire?

PHILO: Through the air!

TOLMAN: Electric light waves moving through air?

PHILO: Just like a Marconi box. A radio transmitter picks up sound waves, and you can hear them. This picks up tiny bits of light, and they are transformed into images inside the vacuum tube.

TOLMAN: So one could look into the tube and see something. A picture, even.

PHILO: More than a picture... movement!

TOLMAN: In other words, a movie not projected on a screen, but radiating from within a glass tube.

PHILO: Yes! Of course, the tube will have to be made larger and flattened so you can see the images easier. I figure a rectangular tube with a ten-inch screen might work. Then you have to modify a camera that could take the picture, break it up into tiny pieces of light, and then send it to the tube.

TOLMAN: Fascinating!

PHILO: Of course, it's all just on paper now. But I think if I experiment more with vacuum tubes and electricity, I might... *(Doubtful.)* I might have something.

TOLMAN: You might indeed!

PENNECOTT: *(ENTERS LEFT with AGNES, who wears a period cheerleader outfit.)* There he is, Agnes. Up to his usual witchcraft.

AGNES: Philo, it's time to go home. Cheerleading practice is over.

PHILO: In a minute...

TOLMAN: Miss Pennecott, Philo has been showing me some extraordinary ideas.

AGNES: More science stuff?

PHILO: Yes.

PENNECOTT: *(To AGNES.)* Your brother will blow up the whole school someday. *(AGNES laughs.)*

TOLMAN: *(Holds up one of the sheets.)* This is remarkable stuff for someone only— How old are you, Philo?

AGNES: He's fifteen!

TOLMAN: Really remarkable!

AGNES: Oh, Philo has always been an egghead.

PENNECOTT: Agnes Farnsworth, what a thing to say about your own brother!

TOLMAN: I fear, Miss Pennecott, that every scientist is, in one way or the other, an egghead.

PENNECOTT: *(Pompous.)* I wouldn't call Mr. Thomas Edison an... egghead.

AGNES: How about Benjamin Franklin? He flew a kite in a thunderstorm!

TOLMAN: Definitely egghead material. *(AGNES laughs.)*

PENNECOTT: *(Offended.)* Really, Mr. Tolman! The things you say sometimes!

AGNES: Besides, Philo isn't a scientist. He's a sophomore! *(Laughs at her own joke.)*

TOLMAN: If he's not a scientist yet, he certainly will become one. Isn't that right, Philo?

PHILO: *(Quiet.)* I... I hope so.

PENNECOTT: Until that time, I suggest you make a greater effort to write the English language more effectively.

AGNES: Come on, Philo. We've got to go.

PENNECOTT: And I have more papers to correct. My boarding house is so noisy that I can never give my grading its full attention there.

TOLMAN: Good afternoon, Miss Pennecott.

AGNES/PHILO: Good afternoon, Miss Pennecott. *(PENNECOTT EXITS LEFT.)*

PHILO: So what do you think, Mr. Tolman? About my project? Do you think it's already been done before?

TOLMAN: Not to my knowledge, Philo. You must continue to work on it. You must!

PHILO: I plan to, Mr. Tolman. *(Gathers up his papers.)*

AGNES: Maybe Philo will finally invent something that will make us rich! Then the whole family can move to Salt Lake City! Or Denver even!

TOLMAN: What Philo has is a very intriguing theory. It might lead to anything.

PHILO: Or it could just end up a theory.

AGNES: *(Disappointed.)* Shucks!

TOLMAN: What do you call your theory, Philo?

PHILO: I hadn't thought about a name. Something to do with telegraphing.

AGNES: They've already invented the telegraph!

TOLMAN: Not just telegraphing messages. Visual images! How about "tele-vision"?

PHILO: Tele-vision?

TOLMAN: Why not? There's the telegraph, the telephone... why not the television?

PHILO: *(Thinks about it.)* Television...

AGNES: That's a stupid name. Let's go, Philo! *(Grabs PHILO'S arm and pulls him to the door.)* We've got to get home!

PHILO: Goodbye, Mr. Tolman. And thanks! *(EXITS LEFT with AGNES.)*

TOLMAN: *(Calls after them.)* See you in class tomorrow! *(Pause. To himself.)* Television. *(Smiles. BLACKOUT.)*

AFTERMATH

Philo Farnsworth continued his study of science at Brigham Young University and took out his first of many patents for an early form of television in 1922. By 1927, he had patented the video tube and video camera, and in the 1930s he experimented with a broadcasting system in Los Angeles. But inventors at Radio Corporation of America (RCA) built on Farnsworth's ideas and perfected them, beginning the first television broadcasts in 1939. Farnsworth spent the rest of his life trying to get the recognition (and the money) he deserved for his original invention. In one court case, he produced his high school charts and diagrams to prove how he had first come up with the concept years before RCA began working on television. Justin Tolman testified on his behalf. Farnsworth won the case and a modest settlement, but his investments and businesses were unsuccessful. When he died in 1971 at the age of sixty-four, Farnsworth was bankrupt and forgotten. Not until television history began to be studied in the later 1970s was Farnsworth revealed to be, and honored as, the true inventor of television.

Lamb Chops and Pineapple

(1927)

BACKGROUND

Born Vilma Koncsics near the turn of the twentieth century in what is now Hungary, Vilma Bánky was a well-known silent film actress in Europe. American film producer Samuel Goldwyn brought her to California to star in Hollywood silent movies, billing her as "The Hungarian Rhapsody." She played opposite the biggest stars of the era, including Ronald Colman and Rudolph Valentino. In 1927, she married the popular American leading man Rod La Rocque, and their wedding was considered the most lavish yet seen in Hollywood. By 1927, Banky was highly acclaimed for her screen acting and was earning over $5,000 a week appearing in American films.

SETTING

TIME: Summer 1927.

PLACE: A farm in southern California where the silent movie *Allegheny Alice* is being filmed.

CHARACTERS

HENRY KING (M) .... film director

ROD LA ROCQUE (M) .... Hollywood leading man

MOLLY (F) .... script girl

VILMA BÁNKY (F) .... famous silent film actress

BILLY (M) .... cameraman

MR. MURDOCK (M) .... assistant producer

SET DESCRIPTION

A fence spans the UPSTAGE, ending at a tree RIGHT. DOWN LEFT, a primitive movie camera is set up next to three camp chairs and a stool.

PROPERTIES

Script (MOLLY).

FLEXIBLE CASTING NOTE

MOLLY, BILLY, and MR. MURDOCK could be played by either gender with only minor script adjustments.

LIGHTS UP on the silent movie film set. Next to the fence under a tree, ROD LA ROCQUE holds VILMA BÁNKY in his arms. She is dressed in an all-American gingham dress and bonnet. She is short with dark hair. ROD is dressed in rugged farm laborer's clothes and wears a hat. He is tall and very handsome. Director HENRY KING and the script girl, MOLLY, sit in two camp chairs DOWN LEFT. Next to them, the cameraman, BILLY, stands behind the camera, looking through the lens and cranking the handle. The film crew wears casual 1920s clothes and hats.

KING: Closer... Hold her closer... Vilma, turn your head away... more... Now, Rod, put your hand on her cheek... gently! Gently! That's good... Now tell her!

ROD: *(In a slight Chicago accent.)* I love you! I love you! I love you!

KING: Vilma, cast your eyes downward... good! Keep talking to her, Rod.

ROD: I love you! I love you! I love you!

KING: Stop! *(BILLY stops cranking.)* Is that all you can come up?

ROD: I'm an actor. Not a writer.

KING: Molly, what's the title card say?

MOLLY: *(Reads from the script.)* "Ever since I first saw you, Miss Alice, I knew you must be mine!"

KING: That's not much better, but all right. Action! *(BILLY cranks.)*

ROD: Ever since I first saw you, Miss Alice, I knew you must be mine!

KING: Vilma, don't look at him yet... think it over... Keep your eyes down... that's good... Now look at him! Right in the eye! Great! Now tell him!

VILMA: *(In a thick Hungarian accent.)* You mest not say sooch tings to me, Chauny!

KING: Stop! *(BILLY stops cranking.)* What's that? Is that the line?

VILMA: Ist da right line, Meester King. I memberize it!

KING: *(To MOLLY.)* What's the title card say?

MOLLY: "You must not say such things to me, Johnny."

VILMA: Dats vat I say! You mest not say sooch tings to me, Chauny!

KING: Okay, okay. Let's try it again from Rod's line. Action! *(BILLY cranks.)*

ROD: Ever since I first saw you, Miss Alice, I knew you must be mine!

KING: Now don't look at him yet… keep looking down… good… Put your hand on her cheek… right… Now look at him, Vilma… good… Now speak…

VILMA: You mest not say sooch tings to me, Chauny!

KING: All right, I guess… Now both of you stare into each other's eyes… closer… yes, that's good… Now your line, Rod…

ROD: I love you! I love you! I love you!

KING: Stop! *(BILLY stops cranking.)* I can read your lips, and they're all wrong. Molly, what's the title card say?

MOLLY: *(Reads from script.)* "I must say what is in my heart."

KING: Yeah. That's better, I guess.

VILMA: Rudney, darlink. Meebe you do like Meester Goldwyn tells me ven I fist come to America.

ROD: What's that?

VILMA: Meester Goldwyn, he seez to me, "Vilma, when dos newspepper reporters ahsk you qvestions und you knows no Inglisch, you must seez to dem, 'Lemb chips und peenapple!'"

KING: What?

VILMA: "Lemb chips und peenapple!"

ROD: *(To KING.)* Lamb chops and pineapple.

MOLLY: Really?

VILMA: Ist truth. So I always say, "Lemb chips und peenapple!" Of curse, dat vas beck befur I lern Inglisch.

KING: You don't say. Okay. Let's get this scene in the can. Billy!

BILLY: The sun has moved too much, Mr. King. We'll have to change the set up and start over.

KING: The whole scene?

BILLY: If you want it to match.

KING: Molly, how much have we got to shoot here?

MOLLY: About five more pages, Mr. King.

KING: Hell! Okay, Billy, set it up.

BILLY: Yes, Mr. King. *(Moves the camera to another position.)*

VILMA: Vat is happenink, Rudney?

ROD: We have to reshoot the scene, dear.

VILMA: Vy?

ROD: The sun.

KING: Oh, hell! Here comes Murdock. And we're a half a day behind. *(MURDOCK ENTERS LEFT. He is a gruff, blunt man.)*

Afternoon, Murdock. We're setting up for the barnyard scene. Almost ready there, Billy?

BILLY: Just about, Mr. King.

MURDOCK: Pack it up, Billy, and get back to the studio. Molly, there's a rewrite meeting in J. R.'s office in twenty minutes. You'll be needed there.

KING: What's going on here? I've got a scene to shoot!

VILMA: Vee not evan git to da kees yet!

MURDOCK: Kiss your husband on your own time.

KING: Murdock, what are you up to?

MURDOCK: Goldwyn has canceled the picture.

VILMA: Canselled my picture? Reeditchulous!

KING: What's happening?

MURDOCK: It's *The Jazz Singer*. Sound! That's what's happening. Goldwyn wants to reshoot *Allegheny Alice* as a talkie. Billy... Molly... get going.

BILLY/MOLLY: Yes, sir. *(EXIT LEFT.)*

VILMA: Who is she, dis talkie?

ROD: Movies that talk, dear.

VILMA: Reeditchulous!

KING: *Allegheny Alice* as a talkie? I see trouble ahead.

MURDOCK: Goldwyn is bringing out a playwright from New York to work on the script. Also, he wants to add a few songs. And other changes.

VILMA: Vat udder chansees, Meester Moodock?

MURDOCK: *(Evasive.)* Oh, you know. Changes.

ROD: Casting changes?

MURDOCK: Maybe.

KING: I knew it! Jolson sings a few songs on screen, and the whole movie business goes crazy!

VILMA: Ay reefuge to zing zongs!

MURDOCK: Oh, you won't be singing any songs, Miss Bánky. I can promise you that.

ROD: Goldwyn's going to replace my Vilma, isn't he?

MURDOCK: Well, of course! I mean, just listen to that accent of hers!

VILMA: Vat aksunt?

MURDOCK: Little Alice Nolan living on the farm in the Allegheny hills. The all-American girl! But when she opens her mouth to speak, we're in Budapest!

KING: The silly story might as well take place in Hungary. It's stupid!

ROD: Miss Bánky has a contract!

MURDOCK: Yeah. Five thousand smackers a week. Don't I know it.

VILMA: Vat aboot my fanz? Thawsuns of dem!

MURDOCK: They better learn Hungarian if they want to understand anything you say.

KING: I'm going to see Goldwyn! He can't do this!

MURDOCK: He's on sound stage three. They're canceling the Bible film and six others. All of them are going to be talkies.

KING: Insanity! *(To ROD and VILMA.)* Don't you two worry. I'll take care of this!

VILMA: Sank you, Meester Kink.

ROD: We really appreciate it, Mr. King.

KING: Come along, Murdock. Sound movies! As Vilma says, "Reeditchulous!" *(EXITS LEFT.)*

MURDOCK: I'm sorry, Miss Bánky. I truly am.

VILMA: I sink I too am surrey. *(MURDOCK EXITS LEFT.)*

ROD: This is bad, my dear. Very bad.

VILMA: Very bed?

ROD: Yes. These talkies are going to ruin us.

VILMA: Boot, Rudney, you speck Inglisch so vell. You con mick talkies!

ROD: I don't want to make movies without you. *(Holds her.)* Oh, my dearest wife, my favorite leading lady! What will we do?

VILMA: Meebee I lernt da beture Inglisch? *(Recites.)* "Lemb chips und peenapple! Lemb chips und peenapple!"

ROD: I've got a better idea. You can go back to Hungary! We both can go together! You will be a star there again as you once were. You can make all the talkies you want in Budapest!

VILMA: Ah, my deerest Rudney. You ist so kind. Boot vat vill you do un Hungree? You vill be da voon vit da aksunt.

ROD: I don't care about my career. You can work there, and we will be happy together!

VILMA: You ist so schveet, my darlink! Boot no. Vee vill schtay reet here un Hollyvood. Vee vill du vat vee can, my darlink. Vee vill soovive, I proomish you!

ROD: I love you! I love you! I love you!

VILMA: No, no. Say "Lemb chips und peenapple! Lemb chips und peenapple!" *(They kiss. BLACKOUT.)*

AFTERMATH

Vilma Bánky's career ended soon after the arrival of talking pictures. She made only four sound films in Hollywood before going back to Europe in 1930 and making a German movie. She retired from movies three years later. Her husband Rod La Rocque continued to make movies up until 1941 and remained with her, living in relative obscurity, until his death in 1969. Bánky died in 1991 but was so forgotten by Hollywood that her passing was not realized nor reported until the following year.

BREAD AND SOUP
(1933)

BACKGROUND

When Franklin D. Roosevelt was elected president in the fall of 1932, the United States was in the depths of the Great Depression. Unemployment was at 24.9%, banks had failed, farms were repossessed, and morale was at its lowest point. In many cities, the homeless and jobless lived in makeshift shantytowns in parks and vacant lots. The shantytowns were called Hoovervilles, named after Herbert Hoover, who was president when the stock market crashed in 1929. Roosevelt was elected with the promise of establishing a better economic outlook and recovering from the Depression.

SETTING

TIME: A cold February morning in 1933.
PLACE: The sidewalk outside a soup kitchen in New York City.

CHARACTERS

LOUIE (M)..................................... rough fellow
CHARLES (M).............................. dapper gent
ESTELLE (F)................................ faded blonde
WILBUR (M) .... her husband
MARTY (M)................................. muscular veteran
ANGEL (F).................................... tough girl in her late teens
MOLLY (F).................................... volunteer at the soup kitchen

SET DESCRIPTION

The door to the soup kitchen is UP RIGHT, with the backdrop being the kitchen's windows, which are covered with old newspapers and a handmade sign that says "Bread and Soup."

PROPERTIES

Baby wrapped in a blanket (ESTELLE); blanket (ANGEL); pocket watch (CHARLES).

SOUND EFFECTS

Baby cries.

LIGHTS UP on a line of six people starting at the door UP RIGHT and stretching LEFT. Closest to the door is CHARLES, who is dressed in a suit that is a bit faded. Next is LOUIE, a loud man wearing a jacket and a cap, followed by ESTELLE, wearing a worn coat and carrying a baby wrapped in a blanket. Her husband, WILBUR, a somber man with a dazed look, stands behind her. MARTY, a gruff man wearing an old Army jacket, is next, followed by ANGEL, a hardened girl who has a faded blanket wrapped around her shoulders. ALL are cold and tired.

LOUIE: Hey, Mac, what time did you get here to be first in line?

CHARLES: Precisely at seven-o'-one.

LOUIE: Yeah? I didn't get here 'til... like... seven thirty, I guess. I ain't got a watch no more.

CHARLES: You arrived at seven thirty-four.

LOUIE: Ya don't say? And what time is it now? If I ain't gettin' too personal.

CHARLES: *(Pulls out a pocket watch.)* Precisely seven fifty-three.

LOUIE: Hey, that's a classy-lookin' timepiece you got there.

CHARLES: It was my father's. And his father's before him.

LOUIE: A regular family heirloom. I had a pretty good watch once. I hocked it back in twenty-nine. Don't need a watch these days. Just get to the bread line early, that's all I need to know.

CHARLES: I believe this is a soup kitchen. Not a bread line.

LOUIE: Sometimes they got soup. Sometimes just bread. You ain't a regular here, are you?

CHARLES: No. The bread line—er—the soup kitchen I frequented on the West Side closed.

LOUIE: No kiddin'?

ESTELLE: The one on Lexington?

CHARLES: Yes.

ESTELLE: Wilbur and me used to go there. It was quite a hike. Weren't it, Wilbur?

WILBUR: I suppose so.

ESTELLE: This place is closer. Of course, the one near Union Square is even closer to us. But that place is always so crowded. And a lot of bums go there. Ain't that right, Wilbur?

WILBUR: I suppose so.

MARTY: Hey, lady, watch what you say. Some of them so-called bums are veterans of the Great War. Like myself.

LOUIE: You don't say.

MARTY: Fourth U.S. Artillery. In France. I did my bit.

ESTELLE: I bet you seen some awful things in the war.

MARTY: Makes this Depression look like a picnic.

CHARLES: Some picnic.

MARTY: I could've been a career man in the Army. They was thinkin' of me for sergeant.

LOUIE: No kiddin'. Maybe you should've done it. They feed you in the Army.

MARTY: Yeah. But my mother was sick, and I had to come back, and... Ah, it ain't worth thinkin' about now.

ESTELLE: Wilbur's mother lived with us 'til the baby came. Ain't that right, Wilbur?

WILBUR: I suppose so.

MARTY: I did pretty good. I got me a job right away. Driving a truck. Made some good money until... you know.

CHARLES: We certainly do.

LOUIE: Hey, Mr. Gold Pocket Watch—

CHARLES: Brass, actually.

LOUIE: Yeah. What did you do before the crash?

CHARLES: Worked in a bank.

MARTY: A banker! Oooh!

LOUIE: You must have seen a lot of money.

CHARLES: Saw it, yes. I was a teller, but the bank failed.

MARTY: Ain't that just like a bank? A little panic, and they go belly up!

ESTELLE: This ain't no little panic. Wilbur's whole shift at the warehouse got fired. Ain't that right, Wilbur?

WILBUR: I suppose so.

ESTELLE: *(In a loud whisper to LOUIE.)* Wilbur didn't take it so good. Tried to kill himself with the oven. Gas, you know. But we don't talk about it.

LOUIE: Yeah? I drove a cab. Eight years.

MARTY: You don't see many cabs like you used to.

LOUIE: Yeah, tell me about it.

ESTELLE: Cabs! We ain't got the money for the streetcar! We walk. Not that there's any place to go. Just this place.

CHARLES: Thank you, Mr. Hoover.

MARTY: You reckon it's all his fault?

CHARLES: His administration was financially suspect.

MARTY: Spoken like a banker!

ESTELLE: Well, if it weren't Hoover's fault, whose was it?

MARTY: Hell if I know. Maybe this Roosevelt fellow can fix things.

CHARLES: Fix things?

MARTY: Yeah, you know. Jobs and stuff. Open the factories. Help the farms.

ANGEL: The farms are dead.

LOUIE: She can talk!

ANGEL: And the farmers are dead!

MARTY: What's a young kid like you know about farms?

ANGEL: 'Cause I run away from one. That's why.

ESTELLE: You run away from home, honey? You oughtn't have done that. A person needs a family in these hard times. Ain't that right, Wilbur?

WILBUR: I suppose so.

ANGEL: Things were so bad, you couldn't get enough for your crop to pay your taxes. I didn't wait around for the bank to foreclose. One night, I run off, and I haven't been back since.

ESTELLE: Why did you come here?

ANGEL: To get a job.

LOUIE: A job! *(ALL laugh.)*

MARTY: You sure came to the wrong place!

ANGEL: I won't go back! I'll find something. Eventually.

ESTELLE: You got a place to stay, honey?

ANGEL: Well...

LOUIE: They got some spaces in the Hooverville in Bryant Park. It ain't the Ritz, but—

CHARLES: The Hooverville in Central Park is much nicer.

MARTY: You don't say?

CHARLES: I should know. I live there.

LOUIE: You? Mr. Gold Watch in a Hooverville?

CHARLES: Brass!

MARTY: Gee, that's tough. I got a room over a garage on Houston Street.

ESTELLE: We're living with Wilbur's mother in Hell's Kitchen. It's a one-bedroom apartment she took up when she moved out from our place. Somehow, we manage. Don't we, Wilbur?

WILBUR: I suppose so.

LOUIE: I got a room in a boarding house on Jane Street. Ain't paid rent in months, but the landlady is a good old girl. As long as I play pinochle with her every night, she don't kick me out.

MARTY: *(Looks OFF LEFT.)* Gee. Look how long the line is now.

LOUIE: They oughta be openin' soon.

CHARLES: *(Checks his watch.)* In precisely two minutes.

ANGEL: *(To MARTY.)* Hey, mister. You think this Roosevelt will create some jobs?

CHARLES: Very unlikely.

MARTY: You never know. He seems like a right smart fellow.

LOUIE: He don't get to be president until next month.

CHARLES: Then what can he do? Nothing! Before you know it, my home shall be known as a Rooseveltville.

ESTELLE: And this soup kitchen will be known as the Stork Club! *(ALL laugh.)*

MARTY: I hope they got soup with vegetables today. I'm getting pretty sick of just onions.

LOUIE: And potato soup!

ESTELLE: Wilbur's mom made a good onion soup. In the old days. Before she got soft in the head. Remember, Wilbur?

WILBUR: I suppose so.

ESTELLE: Onion soup with lots of cheese!

ANGEL: Stop talking about food! *(Starts to cry.)* Please...

ESTELLE: It's okay, honey. I know how you feel. We ain't had a decent meal since... since forever. Here I am trying to nurse little Suzanne here, but unless I get a little something to eat every day, I don't know if I can.

ANGEL: She's very quiet.

ESTELLE: Oh, Suzanne's a good baby. Never cries hardly, even when she's hungry, which is all the time.

LOUIE: I know the feeling.

ESTELLE: What's your name, honey?

ANGEL: Angel.

MARTY: Angel? What kind of name is that?

ANGEL: It's my stage name!

ESTELLE: Oh, you work on the stage?

ANGEL: I hope to.

LOUIE: You sing and dance and stuff like that?

ANGEL: A little. But I want to be an actress. A serious actress.

ESTELLE: Like Greta Garbo!

ANGEL: She's a movie actress. I want to be on the stage.

CHARLES: Like Ethel Barrymore. I saw her once.

MARTY: You figure you're pretty enough to be on the stage?

ANGEL: They don't want glamour girls.

MARTY: They do at Minsky's! *(Some of them laugh.)*

ESTELLE: I think you're pretty, Angel, in a certain way.

LOUIE: Yeah. I bet you'll clean up fine.

CHARLES: Stop encouraging the girl!

LOUIE: What's your problem, Mr. Gold Watch?

CHARLES: Brass! You shouldn't give her false hopes.

ESTELLE: You gotta have some kind of hope these days. Ain't that right, Wilbur?

WILBUR: *(Very definite.)* No.

ESTELLE: No? What's got into you?

WILBUR: No hope. Not for any of us!

MARTY: Hey, that's no way to talk!

CHARLES: Wilbur is right. No hope for any of us!

LOUIE: *(To CHARLES.)* I'm getting fed up with you, buster!

WILBUR: *(Shouts.)* No hope! No hope! No hope!

ESTELLE: Oh, goodness. He's off again!

WILBUR: Stop hoping and die!

ESTELLE: Wilbur, you behave yourself! *(SOUND EFFECT: BABY CRIES.)*

MARTY: Gone cuckoo. I seen it in the war—

ESTELLE: Don't you call my husband cuckoo!

WILBUR: Die! Die! Die!

CHARLES: No hope! No hope! No hope!

LOUIE: Now don't you start—!

WILBUR: Die! Die! Die!

ESTELLE: *(Shouts.)* Wilbur, you stop that! *(The OTHERS start shouting, and a brawl is interrupted by the door opening. MOLLY,* *a cheerful woman, ENTERS from the soup kitchen. ALL quiet down, and the BABY STOPS CRYING.)*

MOLLY: Sorry we're late. We were hoping for some soup from Madison Square, but they ran out yesterday. But we just got in some bread from a bakery uptown. And it's only two days old! So come in from the cold. *(Holds the door open, talking to the OTHERS as they shuffle forward.)* No soup today, folks. But nice bread...

LOUIE: *(To CHARLES.)* I told you it was a bread line. *(LIGHTS FADE OUT as they EXIT through the door.)*

AFTERMATH

Franklin D. Roosevelt was inaugurated as the thirty-second President of the United States on March 4, 1933. In his inaugural speech, he declared, "...the only thing we have to fear is fear itself." The next day, he assembled both Houses of Congress and announced a four-day bank holiday, closing all banks and allowing him to push through the Emergency Banking Act in order to stabilize banking in the country and stop banks from failing. Other acts and programs followed, collectively called the New Deal. Slowly the American economy started to recover. Still, the Depression continued until 1942, when the nation had entered World War II.

LADY LINDY
(1937)

BACKGROUND

Amelia Earhart was born in Atchison, Kansas, in 1897, and was a bit of a tomboy as a child, interested in hobbies like collecting insects and building things. She contracted and survived the Spanish Flu in 1918 but had physical ailments all her life because of it. Although she studied medicine at Columbia University, her primary interest was in aviation, and she started flying in the early 1920s. In 1928, Earhart was the first woman to fly across the Atlantic Ocean, but she was not one of the pilots. All the same, the flight made her famous, and she used her popularity to promote aviation in America. In 1932, she was the first woman to fly solo across the Atlantic. In 1937, she was the first to fly over the Pacific Ocean from California to Honolulu. With her mechanic and co-pilot, Fred Noonan, Earhart set off from California in 1937 to circumnavigate the globe going east, making fueling stops along the way. She was near the last leg of her journey when her plane, a Lockheed Model 10 *Electra*, landed in Lae, New Guinea in the South Pacific to take on fuel.

SETTING

TIME: The evening of July 2, 1937.

PLACE: The interior of a metal shed next to a landing field in Lae, New Guinea.

CHARACTERS

AMELIA EARHART (F) .... famous aviatrix
FRED NOONAN (M) .... her mechanic and co-pilot

SET DESCRIPTION

The interior of the shed is furnished with a table, a few chairs, and a cabinet. The room is lit by an oil lamp on the table. Charts sit on the table next to the lamp. The door to the shed is RIGHT and is wide open, showing that it is dark outside. An overhead fan is on.

PROPERTIES

Ruler (AMELIA); large kerchief (FRED).

LIGHTS UP on AMELIA, standing over the table looking at charts. She wears a pilot's one-piece outfit but nothing on her head, where she sports short hair. She uses a ruler to measure distances on the charts. FRED ENTERS RIGHT. He also wears a pilot's outfit, and he also wears an airman's hat. He wipes the sweat off his forehead with a large kerchief.

FRED: I can't wait to get airborne and away from this heat. One of the field men says it's a hundred six out there… and it's nearly midnight!

AMELIA: Whatever happened to those South Pacific breezes you read about all the time in books?

FRED: Fiction books.

AMELIA: Did you supervise the fueling, Fred?

FRED: Every drop.

AMELIA: Good, because I think we're going to need every last drop. Come look at this.

FRED: *(Crosses to her.)* Is there a problem?

AMELIA: I don't know. You've charted our route to Howland Island north-northeast. Won't that put us west of the island instead of coming in from the south?

FRED: Howland is a skinny piece of land. Less than seven thousand feet long and pretty narrow.

AMELIA: Just long enough to make a clean landing?

FRED: Just. So I thought we better approach it from the west so we have a better chance of seeing it. We can then circle round to get the right angle to land.

AMELIA: They have enough fuel for us on such a tiny island?

FRED: Not normally. But the *Itasca* docked there two days ago and left us plenty.

AMELIA: *(Stares at the chart, shakes her head.)* Two thousand five hundred fifty-six miles.

FRED: Give or take a mile. You can never totally trust the coordinates on these remote islands.

AMELIA: We've never done more than two thousand miles over water on this trip.

FRED: You did more than that when you flew over the Atlantic.

AMELIA: That was the Atlantic. Despite its name, I don't trust the Pacific. Too many open spaces.

FRED: The weather forecast, for what it's worth, is good. I think we might do it in eighteen hours.

AMELIA: Eighteen hours. If we take off at midnight, we ought to get there a few hours before sunset.

FRED: That's the idea.

AMELIA: Fred, I wish this leg of the trip was over. I wish the whole "circle the globe" nonsense was over.

FRED: Homesick?

AMELIA: I miss George, I know that. And he misses me. Each trip it gets worse.

FRED: With all the publicity the great George Putnam is getting out of this flight, I think he'll do okay.

AMELIA: Don't be smug about George. I know you don't like him.

FRED: I only like flyers. Not publishers who sell stories about flyers.

AMELIA: Poor George. What kind of a wife he must think I am.

FRED: The great George Putnam knew you were a flyer from the start. I think he married you because you were a flyer. "Lady Lindy," they called you. I'll bet Putnam came up with that title.

AMELIA: Some other newsman, I think. I can't recall who.

FRED: Well, it sure sold newspapers and magazines and—

AMELIA: Enough, Fred. *(Goes to the door and looks out.)* What time is it?

FRED: Six minutes to midnight.

AMELIA: Not a cloud in the sky. Quarter moon off to the west. A beautiful night for flying.

FRED: Yeah.

AMELIA: Fred, do you remember the first time you saw an airplane? I mean, really saw one in action and what it could do?

FRED: I saw a lot of the early models when I was at sea all those years. The pilots used to pretend to dive bomb us. Just showing off. They were mostly stunt pilots.

AMELIA: The same thing sort of happened to me. A girl friend and I went to see an airshow in Toronto. We weren't in the crowd but watched from this hill nearby. One of the stunt pilots in a triplane saw us, two women standing apart from the others, and thought he'd give us a good scare. He circled round, went real low, and headed right toward us. I guess he wanted to see us run like rabbits. I think my friend did. But I just stood there, fascinated by this triplane heading right for me. I knew he'd pull up at the last minute, and he did. I guess I ruined his fun, but for me, it was exhilarating!

FRED: I suppose you were always a fearless fool.

AMELIA: I suppose so. Soon after that, I was determined to fly. I got different jobs—awful jobs, most of them—and raised enough money to take flying lessons. My mother thought I was crazy, but she contributed a few bucks herself.

FRED: I liked flying school. The men there were different from the ones I knew at sea.

AMELIA: Men. All men, I imagine.

FRED: Back in those days, all men.

AMELIA: No flying school for me. I searched out Anita Snook and took lessons from her.

FRED: Good old Netta. She was a real pioneer.

AMELIA: And she was a woman! I idolized her. Though she could be tough. *(Laughs.)* I remember I cut my hair short because that's how she wore her hair! Haven't let it grow out since.

FRED: You learned from the best.

AMELIA: Fred, can you remember the very first time you flew?

FRED: Sure. It was at flight school—

AMELIA: No. I mean alone. Flying solo. Up there by yourself.

FRED: It was in Arizona. I remember I was nervous as a cat.

AMELIA: Not me. I loved it! Up there with nothing but sky around you. Free to go in any direction or any angle. Just you and the air around you! I'll never forget that feeling. I still get it sometimes.

FRED: I sort of know what you mean. But I must still be a seaman at heart, because I'm always thinking direction and keeping on course. For me, flying is a science. Or maybe mathematics.

AMELIA: For me, it's still a thrill. How can I ever give it up?

FRED: Give up flying? You? Never.

AMELIA: I'm going to be forty in a few weeks. I told George this was my last big...

FRED: Stunt?

AMELIA: Flight. After you've flown around the world, what else is there?

FRED: I know you. Your next stunt will be to fly to the moon, if you can figure out how.

AMELIA: *(Laughs.)* Will you be my co-pilot to the moon, Fred?

FRED: Certainly.

AMELIA: No. I think I should stay home and learn how to cook. George would get a kick out of that.

FRED: That's what you said to me after you were the first woman to fly solo across the Atlantic. And again after we flew from California to Hawaii. I don't think cooking is in your future.

AMELIA: *(Laughs.)* I already know how to make chili—an old Kansas recipe.

FRED: I can't see Putnam eating chili.

AMELIA: *(Still laughing.)* Neither can I! *(They both laugh.)* Fred, we've been through so much together. How come I still like you?

FRED: Because I'm a flyer.

AMELIA: That must have something to do with it. And a hell of a navigator, too.

FRED: I'll keep doing the charts if you continue to keep us on course.

AMELIA: Deal.

FRED: *(Rolls up the charts.)* Did you get any sleep?

AMELIA: A few hours this afternoon. Under a palm tree. I thought I was back in California. What about you?

FRED: Not much. Too hot to sleep.

AMELIA: Maybe it will be cooler on Howland Island. A nice soft bed, somewhere.

FRED: Bed? There's nothing there. Probably not even a palm tree.

AMELIA: Oh, well, all it has to have is plenty of gasoline. I'll wait for Hawaii for the nice bed.

FRED: Let's get the *Electra* on the landing strip and warmed up. It's almost time.

AMELIA: Right. *(Heads toward the door.)*

FRED: *(Stops her.)* Amelia...

AMELIA: Yes, Fred?

FRED: Don't ever stop flying.

AMELIA: What?

FRED: I mean it... Lady Lindy.

AMELIA: No chili for George?

FRED: No chili for George.

AMELIA: Just the two of us flying off together... forever?

FRED: Something like that.

AMELIA: We'll see. But for now, it's a skinny little place called Howland Island.

FRED: *(Laughs.)* So skinny that if you blink, you'll miss it!

AMELIA: Then whatever we do, let's not blink! Come on! *(EXITS RIGHT.)*

FRED: *(To himself.)* Lady Lindy. One in a million. *(EXITS RIGHT. LIGHTS FADE OUT.)*

AFTERMATH

Earhart and Noonan took off in the *Electra* at midnight and headed toward Howland Island. Radio contact was lost after twelve hours, and Earhart and Noonan were never heard from again. Since no wreckage or bodies were ever found, the death of the two pilots remains something of a mystery. Over the years, many theories and explanations have been offered, some believing that the *Electra* crashed near a deserted island where Earhart and Noonan perished. One theory states that the *Electra* was shot down by Japanese military, and the co-pilots were later executed as spies. In 1939, Earhart was officially declared dead so that her husband could clear up legal and financial matters.

WE INTERRUPT THIS PROGRAM

(1938)

BACKGROUND

The program *Mercury Theatre on the Air* was a weekly radio show that dramatized classic works of literature. It featured theatre actor-director Orson Welles, who collaborated with others on the scripts and usually played a major character in the live broadcast. The CBS radio series began in July 1938 and, because it was a literary and high-class program that aired at the same time as a more popular show, it did not have a huge following. For the Sunday broadcast on October 30, 1938, Welles decided to dramatize H. G. Wells's classic science fiction book, *The War of the Worlds*, for Halloween. The setting of the story was changed from England to New Jersey, and actual towns and highways were mentioned. The program took the form of a series of radio news bulletins that sounded authentic enough that many listeners thought a Martian invasion was actually happening.

SETTING

TIME: October 30, 1938.

PLACE: The living room of a middle-class home in Monmouth Junction, New Jersey.

CHARACTERS

GRANDMA (F) .... Geraldine's mother-in-law

GERALDINE (F) .... widowed mother

ROY (M) .... Geraldine's fourteen-year-old son

JOSIE (F) .... Geraldine's eleven-year-old daughter

SHARON (F) .... neighbor girl

SET DESCRIPTION

The living room is furnished with a sofa, coffee table, and chairs. Everything is a bit old-fashioned and worn out. The room is decorated with doilies, photos, and knick-knacks. There is a door LEFT to the front porch and an archway RIGHT to the dining room and the rest of the house.

PROPERTIES

Needle and thread, child's dress (GRANDMA); scissors, white bed sheet (GERALDINE).

SOUND EFFECTS

Radio music, radio laughter, applause.

FLEXIBLE CASTING NOTE

ROY, JOSIE, and SHARON could be played by either gender with only minor script adjustments.

LIGHTS UP on GRANDMA, sitting in her favorite chair sewing. Her dress is simple and a bit out-of-date. GERALDINE sits on the sofa cutting holes in a white bed sheet. She wears a more contemporary dress. It's about eight in the evening. SOUND EFFECT: RADIO MUSIC is heard continuously from the dining room OFF RIGHT.

GRANDMA: I don't see why you have to cut up a perfectly good bedsheet just to make a Halloween costume.

GERALDINE: Mother, it's so worn you can see through it! And there are rips everywhere.

GRANDMA: In my day, we mended rips and tears.

GERALDINE: I know that. This sheet has more patches than a quilt.

GRANDMA: What's that supposed to be?

GERALDINE: Josie wants to go out as a ghost tomorrow night. One of the easiest Halloween costumes I've ever had to make.

GRANDMA: A ghost! What next? I suppose Roy wants to dress up like Frankenstein!

GERALDINE: Roy says he's too old to go trick-or-treating anymore.

GRANDMA: All of fourteen years old! He'll be ready for the old folks' home soon!

GERALDINE: What's that you're sewing, Mother?

GRANDMA: I'm letting out the hem on that dress Josie has outgrown. There's a good two inches here in the hem.

GERALDINE: But Josie hates that dress! She couldn't wait to outgrow it.

GRANDMA: It's a perfectly good dress. She'll learn to like it.

GERALDINE: Maybe I can dye it another color.

GRANDMA: Must they play that blasted radio so loud? A person can hardly hear herself think with all that racket!

GERALDINE: *(Calls into the other room.)* Roy! Josie! Come in here, please!

GRANDMA: The worst invention there ever was, the radio.

GERALDINE: Children! Did you hear me? *(ROY and JOSIE ENTER RIGHT. Roy wears dark trousers and an undershirt. Josie wears a casual dress.)*

ROY: What is it?

GERALDINE: How many times have I had to tell you not to play the radio so loud? It hurts your grandmother's ears.

ROY: *(Sulks.)* Sorry.

GERALDINE: And Josie, I want you to try this ghost costume on. I want to make sure it's not too long. You don't want to trip tomorrow night.

JOSIE: Okay. *(Goes over to GERALDINE and puts the sheet over her head.)*

ROY: Hey, Grandma. How come we don't have the radio in the living room like everybody else? There's no comfortable place to sit in the dining room.

GRANDMA: If it were up to me, I'd put the blasted thing in the garage. If we had a garage.

GERALDINE: *(To JOSIE.)* Did I make the eyes too far apart?

JOSIE: I don't think so.

GRANDMA: *(To ROY.)* This is still my house, and I will not have a radio in my living room where one is supposed to sit quietly and relax.

ROY: *(Testy.)* I'll bet if Dad were still alive, he'd let us have the radio in here.

GERALDINE: *(Angry.)* Roy! You apologize to your grandmother right this second.

ROY: *(Sheepish.)* I'm sorry, Grandma.

GRANDMA: If your father were still alive, I suppose a lot of things would be different. But he's gone, and that's the way it is. *(ROY starts toward the dining room.)*

GERALDINE: Roy, I want that radio so quiet that Grandma can't hear it in here.

ROY: Okay. *(EXITS RIGHT.)*

JOSIE: Can you make the mouth bigger, Mom? And don't forget a hole for the nose so I can breathe. *(RADIO MUSIC GETS QUIETER.)*

GERALDINE: Stand still, Josie. I'll make a mark where the nose should go.

JOSIE: Hurry! Charlie McCarthy is just starting!

GRANDMA: And who, pray, is Charlie McCarthy?

JOSIE: He's a dummy, Grandma.

GRANDMA: If he's on the radio, he must be.

GERALDINE: She means that he's a ventriloquist's dummy, Mother. It's the Edgar Bergen-Charlie McCarthy Show.

GRANDMA: A ventriloquist on the radio? How do you know if his lips are moving or not?

JOSIE: Charlie McCarthy is the funniest thing on the radio!

GRANDMA: No doubt he is. A dummy! I rest my case.

GERALDINE: *(To JOSIE.)* There. I think I got it right. *(Takes the sheet off of her.)*

JOSIE: Thanks, Mom! *(Runs OFF RIGHT.)*

GERALDINE: I'm sorry about what Roy said, Mother. I mean about Harold. I know that this is your house, and you were so kind to let us move in here when he died.

GRANDMA: *(Soft.)* I wish Harold was here with us.

GERALDINE: So do I, Mother.

GRANDMA: I suppose everything would be different.

GERALDINE: Perhaps.

GRANDMA: I should have been the one to die of pneumonia, not my son.

GERALDINE: *(Gentle.)* Don't talk that way, Mother.

GRANDMA: That must be what you're all thinking.

GERALDINE: *(Shocked.)* Mother!

GRANDMA: Well, that's what I keep thinking. *(Pause.)* What color?

GERALDINE: Pardon?

GRANDMA: What color are you thinking of dying this dress?

GERALDINE: Oh… *(Thinks.)* Blue, maybe.

GRANDMA: Blue might look nice.

JOSIE: *(ENTERS RIGHT. Whines.)* Mom!

GERALDINE: What's the matter now, Josie?

JOSIE: We're trying to listen to Charlie McCarthy, but whenever a commercial comes on, Roy keeps changing the station!

GERALDINE: You don't want to listen to the commercials, do you?

JOSIE: No. But now there's a lot of talking on the radio, and he won't turn it back to Charlie McCarthy!

GERALDINE: *(Calls OFF RIGHT.)* Roy! Let your sister listen to the Edgar Bergen Show! *(ROY ENTERS RIGHT, looking a bit pale and frightened.)* What's the matter, Roy?

ROY: Mom! They interrupted this other program—I don't know what show it is—but they just announced that a spaceship has landed in Grover's Mills, New Jersey.

GERALDINE: A spaceship?

ROY: From Mars!

GRANDMA: That's ridiculous!

JOSIE: How do they know it's from Mars?

ROY: Because there are Martians coming out of it!

GERALDINE: *(Unsure.)* Roy, that's… silly.

ROY: I'm not kidding! Come and listen for yourself!

GERALDINE: But, Roy—

ROY: Please, Mom!

GRANDMA: You sure it's not that dummy talking?

ROY: I'm serious, Grandma. Please, Mom!

GERALDINE: Very well.

ROY: The newsman has seen the Martians and even described what they look like! *(EXITS RIGHT with GERALDINE.)*

GRANDMA: Martians in Grover's Mills! What next?!

JOSIE: How far away is Grover's Mills, Grandma?

GRANDMA: Oh, about six miles as the crow flies. I don't know how far as Martians fly.

JOSIE: *(Frightened.)* That's close to here, Grandma! What if they come to Monmouth Junction?

GRANDMA: Here? Why would any Martian want to come here?

JOSIE: I'm scared, Grandma!

GRANDMA: Nonsense, Josie! There's nothing to be afraid of. It's just the radio—

GERALDINE: *(ENTERS RIGHT with ROY. In a panic.)* This is serious, Mother! Something awful is going on! The man on the radio says there really are Martians, and they are moving west towards us!

ROY: They called the National Guard to try and stop them! But the Martians have these ray guns and—!

JOSIE: *(Rushes into GERALDINE'S arms.)* Oh, Mommy, I'm scared!

ROY: We've got to get out of here!

GRANDMA: I'm not going anywhere. This is all preposterous!

GERALDINE: But the man on the radio said—!

ROY: We got to head south! Away from the path of the Martians!

JOSIE: But I can't run very fast! I've got a sore knee!

GERALDINE: Who do we know with a car?

ROY: Uncle Louie has a car!

GRANDMA: That's because he's a traveling salesman. Louis is in Connecticut, I think. *(There is a BANGING on the door LEFT. GERALDINE and JOSIE scream.)*

ROY: Who can that be? *(Goes to the front door.)*

GRANDMA: Do Martians knock first? *(ROY opens the door, and SHARON ENTERS LEFT. She wears a coat over her dress.)*

SHARON: Did you folks hear the news?

GERALDINE: Sharon! Are there really Martians heading this way?

SHARON: That's what it said on the radio. Dad and I are going over to the armory! We thought it might be the safest place!

ROY: *(Looks out the door.)* The Landermans are all in their car and pulling out of their driveway!

GRANDMA: Well, there goes the only car on the block. Just like the Landermans!

GERALDINE: *(To ROY.)* Should we go with Sharon to the armory?

GRANDMA: I'm not going to any armory!

SHARON: Hurry if you want to join us! First I've got to find Pebbles! *(EXITS LEFT, and ROY closes the door.)*

GRANDMA: Pebbles! What would the Martians want with that nasty tomcat?

GERALDINE: I don't know what to do!

ROY: I better go and find out the latest on the radio! *(EXITS RIGHT.)*

JOSIE: *(Cries.)* Mommy, I'm so scared!

GRANDMA: Martians in New Jersey! Now I've heard everything! *(SOUND EFFECT: RADIO LAUGHTER AND APPLAUSE.)*

GERALDINE: What is that?

GRANDMA: The Martians. They sound like they're having a good time, too. *(ROY ENTERS RIGHT, slowly.)*

GERALDINE: What's that on the radio, Roy?

ROY: *(Dazed.)* The Edgar Bergen Show.

GERALDINE: What?

ROY: I turned the dial to another station to get more news. And it was Charlie McCarthy talking.

JOSIE: Doesn't Charlie know about the Martians?

ROY: Then I went back to CBS and… *(Hesitates.)*

GRANDMA: And?

ROY: It was just a drama. The whole Martian thing. They said it was just a show for Halloween. *(Long pause. ALL are in a state of shock.)*

GERALDINE: *(Slow.)* Oh, my goodness…

JOSIE: There are no Martians then?

ROY: At least not in New Jersey.

GERALDINE: I'm... speechless...

GRANDMA: *(Matter of fact.)* I hate the radio. *(BLACKOUT.)*

AFTERMATH

CBS radio headquarters in New York City was flooded with hundreds of telephone calls during the one-hour *Mercury Theatre* program—listeners trying to find out if this was news or fiction. There was public panic in some areas, particularly in New Jersey where the Martians had supposedly landed. At the end of the program, Welles announced that the show was just an adaptation of H.G. Wells's fiction novel *War of the Worlds* to celebrate Halloween. The next day there were complaints from viewers, newspapers, and politicians to the Federal Communications Commission about the use of the airwaves to deceive and panic the public. The broadcast made the 23-year-old Orson Welles famous.

POISON

(1939)

BACKGROUND

Alice Hamilton was born in New York City in 1869 into a family of educators. As a child, she excelled in science. She entered the University of Michigan Medical School in 1892 and specialized in occupational health hazards. In 1919, Hamilton was the first woman appointed to the faculty of Harvard University, where she taught in the Department of Industrial Medicine at the university's medical school. She was also very active in health reform, birth control, civil liberties, and women's suffrage. In 1935, Hamilton retired from Harvard and was named medical consultant to the US Department of Labor Standards. At the time of this scene in 1939, Franklin D. Roosevelt was in his sixth year as President of the United States and hoping to keep the country out of any war that broke out in Europe.

SETTING

TIME: The morning of September 1, 1939.

PLACE: The outer office of the Oval Office in the White House.

CHARACTERS

MARGUERITE LEHAND (F) ...... FDR's personal secretary

ALICE HAMILTON (F) .... doctor, research scientist, and retired educator

HARRY HOPKINS (M) .... FDR's chief of staff

SET DESCRIPTION

There is a door to the Oval Office LEFT. In front of it sits a desk with a chair behind it. File cabinets line the UPSTAGE wall, and four chairs for waiting guests sit along the remaining wall space. A door to the hall is RIGHT. Framed historical naval prints hang on the walls. On the desk is a period phone console.

PROPERTIES

Letter (ALICE).

SOUND EFFECTS

Various telephone buzzing sounds.

LIGHTS UP on MARGUERITE at her desk on the phone. She is dressed in a dark suit ensemble with a white blouse. ALICE HAMILTON is standing in front of a historical print hanging on the wall. She is elderly, but far from frail, and dressed in her finest dress and hat, though both are a little old-fashioned for the time.

MARGUERITE: *(Into the phone.)* I'm afraid that won't be possible, Mr. Congressman. His day is fully booked. *(Pause.)* Perhaps you should talk to Mr. Hopkins. *(Pause.)* No, he's with the President at the moment. Try his office a little later. *(Pause.)* Yes, sir... *(Pause.)* I'm sorry, sir. *(Hangs up the phone. To herself.)* Republican pest! *(To ALICE.)* Please make yourself comfortable, Dr. Hamilton. You may want to have a seat. There's no saying how long Mr. Hopkins will be in there with the President.

ALICE: I'm fine, my dear. I am enjoying these lovely historical prints. This one here of the Monitor and the Merrimack is quite interesting. A bit before my time. The Civil War, I mean. I was born during that horrible period they called the Reconstruction. But my parents and all my aunts and uncles knew the Civil War very well. In fact, it seemed that they talked of nothing else. *(Moves to another print.)* Now this one of John Paul Jones aboard the *USS Alfred* is way before my time. My relatives didn't talk much about the Revolutionary War. *(Moves to another print.)* Ah, the *USS Maine* in Havana Harbor. "Remember the *Maine!*" I certainly do remember that. *(Crosses to the desk.)* You must have quite an avid interest in naval military history, my dear.

MARGUERITE: *(Laughs.)* I don't know the first thing about it. These prints all belong to the President. He is the expert on naval history, and he has a passion for boats of any kind.

ALICE: What are they all doing in your office?

MARGUERITE: I think the President ran out of space for all the naval paraphernalia that he owns. The White House is filled with so many nautical things that the Republicans say the place resembles a yacht club! *(Both laugh.)*

ALICE: *(Looks at the prints again.)* Well, I think these are all very nice.

MARGUERITE: I'm just grateful I didn't get stuck with his scale model of Old Ironsides! It's six feet long! *(Both laugh again.)*

ALICE: *(Finally sits.)* Well, my dear, it's a very nice office.

MARGUERITE: It's a very busy office! It seems everyone wants to see the President. Trying to keep his calendar in any kind of order is a nightmare.

ALICE: I hope I am not intruding terribly much.

MARGUERITE: *(Rises.)* Oh, Dr. Hamilton. I didn't mean to imply—

ALICE: I was invited. A formal letter and all. *(Takes out the letter.)* A very gracious invitation to meet with him. He even signed it "Franklin," though we are total strangers.

MARGUERITE: The President is very anxious to meet you. During our meeting this morning, we went over your many accomplishments. Graduated from medical school when you were only twenty-three years old. The first woman to be on the faculty of Harvard. And now you're the chief medical consultant to the US Department of Labor Standards. I am surprised that you and the President have not met before.

ALICE: *(Laughs.)* Well, I don't know his excuse, but I have been quite busy all these years.

MARGUERITE: Today the two of you will finally meet. *(Returns to her desk and sits.)* I just hope we don't keep you waiting very long.

ALICE: I think Eleanor might be behind all this.

MARGUERITE: Mrs. Roosevelt?

ALICE: We've met several times over the years. We share several causes, you know. Civil liberties. Health issues. Even birth control committees. Eleanor says to me every time we meet, "You must talk to Franklin about it!" *(Laughs.)* Well, I guess she finally wore him down!

MARGUERITE: Is that what you want to discuss with the President? Birth control?

ALICE: Oh, I don't think he's quite up to talking about that. Most men aren't. Besides, I'm sure Eleanor has already given him an earful about that subject. No, I would like to discuss toxicology.

MARGUERITE: I'm afraid I'm not quite sure what that is, Dr. Hamilton.

ALICE: Poison. Industrial poison, my dear.

MARGUERITE: Like pollution?

ALICE: Worse than that. Pollution is when harmful chemicals and smoke are released into the air. A terrible thing. But toxicology refers to the poisons that occur in a factory or any other place of manufacture. The men and women working in these places breathe these toxins, as we call them. Breathe them in hour after hour, day after day. The manufacturers look only at the products, not at the unhealthy conditions under which they are made.

MARGUERITE: I see.

ALICE: I have done studies, and the results are frightening. I keep telling the Department of Labor Standards about the problems, but they... well, they have many other concerns to deal with. At least they got the children out of the factories.

MARGUERITE: Yes.

ALICE: Thanks to Mr. Roosevelt, the economy is improving and factories that have been idle for years are now in operation again. This is a good thing, but with it returns the problem of toxicology.

MARGUERITE: I believe the President will be very interested in what you have to say, Doctor.

ALICE: I hope so. But he has so many different problems he has to deal with every day that I fear— *(The door to the Oval Office opens, and HARRY ENTERS through it, closing the door behind him.)*

HARRY: Poor Franklin. He's on the telephone with Senator Huey Long. I wouldn't wish that on my worst enemy.

MARGUERITE: I thought Senator Long was your worst enemy.

HARRY: Come to think of it, Marguerite, he is! *(Laughs.)*

MARGUERITE: Dr. Hamilton, I'd like to introduce you to Harry Hopkins, the President's chief of staff—

HARRY: And all-around dog's body. *(Shakes ALICE'S hand.)* Glad to meet you, Doctor. I know all about your work in the Department of Labor Standards.

ALICE: And everyone knows you, Mr. Hopkins, for your work in... well, just about everything.

HARRY: That's me. All over the place.

MARGUERITE: Dr. Hamilton has been invited here by the President.

HARRY: He's damn busy, but I'm sure he's anxious to meet you, Doctor. Always good to have a Democrat visiting the Oval Office. You are a Democrat, aren't you?

ALICE: Well, I voted for Mr. Roosevelt. Twice!

HARRY: Not in the same election, I hope! *(ALL laugh.)*

ALICE: Mr. Hopkins, I believe you are, as they say, pulling my leg!

HARRY: Just part of the job. *(To MARGUERITE.)* Marguerite, I'll be in my office with Chief Justice Douglas if Franklin asks for me.

MARGUERITE: Yes, Mr. Hopkins.

HARRY: Nice meeting you, Doctor.

ALICE: And you, too, Mr. Hopkins. *(HARRY EXITS RIGHT.)*

MARGUERITE: I hope the President is not on the phone with the Senator much longer. You shouldn't be kept waiting any more than you already have.

ALICE: Don't you worry yourself. I'm fine.

MARGUERITE: Now before you go in to see the President, there are a few things I should tell you. First of all, do not be offended when he doesn't stand up when you enter or come to shake your hand. You just go directly to his desk, and he'll extend his hand to you.

ALICE: That's rather unusual.

MARGUERITE: Not here. You see, the President cannot stand or walk without assistance.

ALICE: What? I've seen him in so many newsreels and—

MARGUERITE: And every time you saw him, he was sitting in a chair or in a car. The President does not want the public to know how serious his infirmity is. He feels it will weaken his position as president. And, of course, he doesn't want sympathy from anyone.

ALICE: You are telling me that the most powerful leader in the world today is crippled? How is that possible?

MARGUERITE: He contracted polio when he was thirty-nine years old.

ALICE: How has he kept such a thing secret?

MARGUERITE: Most members of the press are aware of the situation and have always cooperated. No photos are taken or newsreels filmed until they get the go-ahead from Mr. Hopkins.

ALICE: As a doctor, I am surprised that I never noticed anything. He always seems so healthy and... capable.

MARGUERITE: As a doctor, you know a weak body does not hinder a superior brain.

ALICE: Certainly.

MARGUERITE: The second thing I have to tell you is much more difficult.

ALICE: What is it, my dear?

MARGUERITE: You must not talk about the President's infirmity to anyone. You have been entrusted with a very important secret, and the damage that can be done if this secret is divulged would be considerable.

ALICE: You have my word of honor as a doctor and a citizen.

MARGUERITE: We all appreciate that. Now, the President will most likely smoke a cigarette, and I think his dog Fala is in there with him today. Do not let it bother you. It is best if you sit in the blue chair. The President will indicate it to you. Hopefully, you will not be interrupted by the phone ringing. Only calls of crucial importance will be allowed— *(SOUND EFFECT: BUZZING from the phone on her desk, followed by a second, DIFFERENT BUZZING. Then several more BUZZING SOUNDS.)* What is going on here? *(Looks at her phone console.)* All six lines are lit up!

HARRY: *(Rushes IN RIGHT.)* It's happened! Now all hell is going to break loose!

MARGUERITE: Every line is buzzing! What's happened?

HARRY: Hitler has invaded Poland! Thousands of German troops, planes, tanks… everything! This means war in Europe! *(Crosses to the Oval Office door and opens it, then turns back to MARGUERITE.)* Marguerite, don't even try to put those calls through. And cancel all appointments for the rest of the day! *(EXITS LEFT, closing the door behind him. The phones keep BUZZING.)*

MARGUERITE: War in Europe!

ALICE: *(Rises.)* How dreadful! Do you think Mr. Roosevelt will be able to keep us out of it?

MARGUERITE: He'll do everything he can to maintain neutrality. Oh, but if the Germans have invaded Poland, both France and Great Britain have vowed to declare war on Hitler!

ALICE: *(Sad.)* It means another major war. I hoped I would never live long enough to see such a war again.

MARGUERITE: *(Crosses to ALICE.)* I am so sorry, Dr. Hamilton. There is no way the President can see you today considering—

ALICE: Certainly not. I completely understand, my dear.

MARGUERITE: Thank you, Doctor.

ALICE: *(Crosses to the RIGHT door.)* The problem of toxicology will have to wait for another day. Do you know what is worse than industrial poisons?

MARGUERITE: What's that?

ALICE: Bombs and bullets. Good day, my dear. *(EXITS RIGHT. MARGUERITE returns to her desk and looks at the buzzing phone system with horror. LIGHTS SLOWLY FADE OUT.)*

AFTERMATH

Although Great Britain and France declared war on Germany after Hitler's troops invaded Poland, the United States remained neutral for more than two years after that, until Japan bombed Pearl Harbor. Alice Hamilton remained active, lecturing and writing books on the dangers of industrial toxicology. She died in 1970 at the age of 101.

SUNDAY MORNING
(1941)

BACKGROUND

Relations between the United States and Japan had deteriorated significantly by 1941. All trade with Japan had ceased, and President Roosevelt ordered much of the nation's Pacific naval fleet from San Diego, California, to Pearl Harbor in the Hawaiian island of Oahu. By December of 1941, about 120,000 American soldiers were stationed at the Hawaiian base, some with families living in the nearby city of Honolulu.

SETTING

TIME: Sunday morning, December 7, 1941.
PLACE: The adjoining backyards of two connected family military houses in Honolulu, Hawaii.

CHARACTERS

ADELA (F)...................................... mother and serviceman's wife
STELLA (F)..................................... neighbor woman, slightly older
ROSITA (F) .... Adela's thirteen-year-old daughter
MANUEL (M)............................... her twin brother

SET DESCRIPTION

The backdrop shows houses that are simple and a bit run down. Each has a screen door leading into the house. The yards are small with beat-up lawn chairs. There is a kid's bicycle leaning against the RIGHT house. There is nothing dividing the two yards.

PROPERTIES

Cup of coffee, watch, hat, purse (ADELA); cup of coffee (STELLA); hat, hairbrush (ROSITA); tie (MANUEL).

SOUND EFFECTS

Planes approaching at increasing volumes, distant explosions, planes flying overhead.

LIGHTS UP on ADELA, sitting in a lawn chair RIGHT with a cup of coffee. She is dressed in a presentable dress and high heels. The time is about seven thirty in the morning. She sips her coffee and enjoys the quiet. After a moment, her neighbor STELLA ENTERS from the LEFT screen door. She wears a housedress and slippers and also carries a cup of coffee.

ADELA: *(In Spanish.) Hola!*

STELLA: *Hola* to you, too, Adela. You're up early.

ADELA: *(In a slight Spanish accent.)* It's Sunday. We are going to the eight-thirty mass.

STELLA: It's Sunday already? I lose track. One day's like another in this place. When I had a job back in the States, I always knew what day it was. Not here.

ADELA: With the children going to school and Ramón having such crazy hours at the base, I have to keep track of the days very carefully.

STELLA: Ramón on the night watch again?

ADELA: For two weeks now. He finishes at eight o'clock. If he hurries home, he will be able to go to church with us.

STELLA: Frank got off at midnight last night. He stumbled in here about three in the morning, as loud and plastered as always. He's upstairs now, sleeping it off.

ADELA: I feel so sorry for you, Stella. I really do.

STELLA: All those guys stationed at Pearl with nothing to do but drink and play cards. They need a war or something before they all go stir crazy.

ADELA: Oh, Stella, don't say that! Not a war!

STELLA: Not a big war. Just a little one. Enough to have them go capture an island or something so that they feel like real soldiers.

ADELA: *(Makes the sign of the cross.)* I pray to God that there be no war for us. Not like in Europe. And in China, too.

STELLA: Well, both of those places are so far away from here that we'd be the last to hear about it.

ADELA: *¿Qué hora es? (Looks at her watch.)* Look at the time! *(Crosses to the RIGHT screen door.)* Manuel! Rosita! *¡Apúrate!* Finish your Cheerios and get dressed for church! *¡Apúrate!*

STELLA: If Frank and I had kids, it might be different. Hell, maybe I'd even take them to church, too.

ADELA: *(Still at the door.)* Do you hear me? *¡Apúrate!*

STELLA: On the other hand, Frank would have made one rotten father.

ADELA: *(To STELLA.)* You know, Stella, you are always welcome to come to St. Michael's with us.

STELLA: Thanks, honey. But I think it's too late for me.

ROSITA: *(ENTERS through the RIGHT screen door. She is wearing a pretty dress and hat for church. She has no accent.)* I'm already dressed, Mama!

STELLA: You look beautiful, Rosita!

ROSITA: Thank you, Mrs. Bradley.

STELLA: A new hat?

ROSITA: Well...

ADELA: Rosita, who told you that you can wear one of my hats?

ROSITA: Please? It fits me, Mama!

STELLA: It certainly does.

ADELA: Next time, you ask! Is your brother almost ready?

ROSITA: He's listening to the radio.

ADELA: The radio! *¡Dios mio! (Calls into the house.)* Manuel! Did you hear your mother! *(EXITS RIGHT into the house.)*

STELLA: You're growing up so fast, Rosita. I remember when your family first moved to Honolulu, you were a skinny little thing!

ROSITA: It was only two years ago.

STELLA: Only two? I thought it was longer. How slowly time goes here.

ROSITA: Manuel and I turned thirteen in April. Don't you remember, Mrs. Bradley? You were at our birthday party!

STELLA: Was I? My mind is turning to mush. It's these God-forsaken islands.

ROSITA: Don't you like Hawaii?

STELLA: Not much.

ROSITA: Mama says we are lucky to be here close to Papa. Many families are far away from their papas. Like when we lived in California, and Papa was stationed in Alaska.

STELLA: I guess this place is better than Alaska, but I'm not so sure. We've been here eight years. Eight long years. I'm just about ready for Alaska. Anything different.

ROSITA: Mr. Bradley has been a soldier for a long time, hasn't he?

STELLA: Forever. A career man.

ROSITA: What is a career man?

STELLA: A soldier who never grows up.

ROSITA: I don't think I understand that.

STELLA: Neither do I, Rosita. Neither do I.

ADELA: *(ENTERS RIGHT from the house.)* That boy! He'll drive me *loco* one day!

ROSITA: Manuel is just a teenager, Mama.

ADELA: And what does that make you? An old lady?

ROSITA: We might be twins, but girls are more mature than boys.

STELLA: I'll agree with that.

ADELA: Rosita, you can wear my hat, but your hair is a mess in the back. Go fetch my hairbrush, and I'll make it nice.

ROSITA: Okay. *(EXITS RIGHT into the house.)*

STELLA: How did those two get to be thirteen already?

ADELA: Children grow so fast.

STELLA: Yeah, I must've blinked. Before you know it, Ramón's term will be up, and you'll all get back to civilization.

ADELA: *Sí.* I cannot wait for the day. My family is in Fresno, and my uncle says he can get Ramón a job when he gets out of the service.

STELLA: That's good. A real future. Good to have a future, I say.

ADELA: Also, I do not think Honolulu is a good place to raise children. Too many... people.

STELLA: Too many soldiers, you mean. The city is crawling with them. Frank says there are now over one hundred thousand men at Pearl. That many men with nothing to do on leave but tear up the town. It's not safe to go downtown these days.

ADELA: Sometimes, I worry. Ramón says all the time to be careful. But I have to go to the market, and the dentist for the twins. Even walking to church, I am a little worried. That is why I like it when Ramón is able to come with us.

ROSITA: *(ENTERS RIGHT from the house with a hairbrush.)* Here, Mama.

ADELA: *(Takes off the hat and puts it on the lawn chair.)* It's all tangled up in back. *(Brushes ROSITA'S hair.)* When did you wash it?

ROSITA: Last night.

ADELA: You should have brushed it before you went to bed.

STELLA: Such pretty hair, Rosita. Mine was never that silky. More like steel wool!

ADELA: But you have such nice color in your hair, Stella.

STELLA: It comes out of a bottle.

MANUEL: *(ENTERS RIGHT from the house. He wears dress pants, a white dress shirt with an open collar, and a jacket. He doesn't speak with an accent.)* Do I have to wear a tie? It's so hot today.

ADELA: Of course you have to wear a tie. We're going to church, not the movies.

MANUEL: Some of the guys at St. Michael's don't wear ties.

ROSITA: All the men do. *(ADELA finishes brushing.)*

MANUEL: *(To ROSITA.)* Who asked for your advice?

ROSITA: It's not advice. It's just a fact. The men wear ties, and the ladies wear hats.

MANUEL: Yeah? Where's your hat?

ADELA: Right here. *(Gives ROSITA the hat.)* Go look in the mirror when you put it on so it will be perfect.

ROSITA: Yes, Mama. *(EXITS RIGHT into the house.)*

ADELE: And you, Manuel, go get your blue tie. The nice one. I'll tie it on you.

MANUEL: *(Sulks.)* I know how to tie a tie. *(EXITS RIGHT into house.)*

ADELA: *¡Niños!* They will make me old before my time!

STELLA: You're lucky to have them, and you know it.

ADELA: *Sí.* I should not complain. Especially in front of you, Stella.

STELLA: Don't mind me. I'm just an old sourpuss with nothing good to say about anything. At least that's what Frank says about me.

ROSITA: *(ENTERS RIGHT from the house, wearing the hat.)* How's this?

ADELA: Turn around and let me see. *(ROSITA spins around.)*

STELLA: Beautiful!

ADELA: I cannot believe my hat fits you so well. You are growing up.

STELLA: Pretty soon you can start wearing your mother's dresses.

ROSITA: Those old things! No, thank you!

ADELA: *(Slightly offended.)* Excuse me, I like them.

ROSITA: Well, not old. Just…

ADELA: Just old-fashioned?

STELLA: *(To ROSITA.)* I think your mother is a pretty snazzy dresser.

ADELA: Thank you, Stella.

STELLA: Just because I dress like a slob doesn't mean I don't know style. *(MANUEL ENTERS RIGHT from the house, wearing a tie that isn't blue.)*

ADELA: Let me look at you, Manuel. *(He turns to face her.)* I said the blue tie! The nice one.

MANUEL: I couldn't find it.

ADELA: Well, this will have to do. *(Straightens his tie.)* Once it's straight.

STELLA: Manuel, you look like a real gent. I mean it.

MANUEL: *(Sour.)* Thanks, I guess.

ADELA: *(Looks at her watch.)* ¿Qué hora es? Ten minutes to eight. Now let me get my hat and purse, and we'll be on our way. We'll walk toward Third Avenue—

MANUEL: But that's the long way. And it's so hot!

ADELA: We are going to Third because we might be able to meet up with your father when he gets off duty at eight. *(EXITS RIGHT into the house.)*

ROSITA: I don't think it's so hot.

MANUEL: Who asked you?

STELLA: If you want my opinion, I think the two of you look terrific. And only thirteen. I think someday you both are going to break a lot of hearts! *(SOUND EFFECT: PLANES APPROACHING in the distance.)* But don't tell your mother I said that. *(Smiles.)* Our secret. *(SOUND EFFECT: PLANES GET LOUDER. MANUEL looks up for them.)*

ROSITA: *(Smiles.)* Our secret, Mrs. Bradley.

MANUEL: Look! Air maneuvers!

STELLA: On a Sunday morning? Those pilots must really be bored. *(ADELA ENTERS RIGHT from the house, wearing a hat and carrying a purse.)*

MANUAL: Look, Mama. Maneuvers!

ROSITA: Look at them all.

ADELA: So many planes… *(SOUND EFFECT: PLANES BECOME VERY LOUD.)*

STELLA: Maybe they'll wake up Frank.

MANUEL: Look how low they're flying. They must be landing at the base.

ADELA: All at one time? There are too many. *(SOUND EFFECT: DISTANT EXPLOSIONS heard.)* ¿*Qué pasa?* *(SOUND EFFECT: EXPLOSIONS and PLANES FLYING OVERHEAD.)*

STELLA: Something blew up at the base! Something big!

ADELA: My Ramón! *¡Dios mio!*

MANUEL: Mama! Mrs. Bradley!

STELLA: What is it, Manuel?

MANUEL: Those... those are not our planes!

ADELA: *¡Dios nos ayude!*

STELLA: The kid is right! Those are Jap planes! *(SOUND EFFECT: EXPLOSIONS.)*

ROSITA: *(Frightened.)* What's going on, Mama?

ADELA: I don't know! I don't understand!

STELLA: I think I do. *(Crosses to the LEFT screen door and shouts.)* Frank! Frank, wake up!

MANUEL: It's an attack! They're bombing the base!

ADELA: No! My Ramón!

STELLA: *(Still shouts.)* Frank! Get up! We got visitors! *(SOUND EFFECT: EXPLOSIONS. BLACKOUT.)*

AFTERMATH

Hundreds of Japanese fighter planes attacked Pearl Harbor just before eight o'clock the morning of December 7, 1941. During the two-hour attack, the Japanese destroyed twenty American naval vessels, including eight full-size battleships, and more than three hundred American aircraft. The surprise attack killed over two thousand American soldiers and sailors and wounded another one thousand. The next day, President Roosevelt asked Congress to declare war on Japan, and Congress approved the declaration. On December 11, Japan, Germany, and Italy declared war on the United States. After more than two years of remaining isolated from the wars in Europe and the Pacific, America was actively involved in World War II.

ADD ONE CUP OF SUGAR

(1943)

BACKGROUND

After America entered World War II in December of 1941, global trading was affected, and there were shortages of products just about everywhere. In the United States, the Food Rationing Program was instituted in 1942, and by the next year, many items were in short supply. Coffee, sugar, gasoline, rubber tires, meats, butter, cooking oil, and even shoes and other clothing items were only available if one had rationing coupons, which were distributed equally to families. Sugar was particularly difficult to get and sugar coupons were very valuable.

SETTING

TIME: August 1943.

PLACE: A kitchen in an apartment in the Bronx, New York City.

CHARACTERS

WILBUR (M) .... husband with a mental disorder

ESTELLE (F) .... his wife

MARTHA (F) .... neighbor woman

SUZANNE (F) .... Wilbur's ten-year-old daughter

SET DESCRIPTION

The kitchen is small, but clean and orderly. A stove with a coffee pot sits along the RIGHT wall. An "ice box" refrigerator sits along the UPSTAGE wall next to a sink, counter, and cabinets. There is a sugar bowl with a spoon in one of the cabinets. A table with a coffee cup on it sits DOWN LEFT. Three chairs surround the table. A door LEFT leads to the outside hall, and an archway RIGHT leads to the rest of the apartment.

PROPERTIES

Purse, hat, pink dress, sugar bowl (ESTELLE).

LIGHTS UP on WILBUR, standing in front of the stove and staring at a coffee pot. (We've met Wilbur and his family before, in the *Bread and Soup* scene [1933].) He is now in his late forties but looks much older. His face is drawn and pale, he moves and talks slowly, and he often seems confused. He wears trousers, suspenders, and a white undershirt. It is six o'clock in the evening. After a time, he finally pours some coffee into a cup sitting on the table. Replacing the pot on the stove, he sits in one of the chairs and stares at the coffee cup. Finally he tries to drink it.

WILBUR: Too hot. The coffee is too hot... *(Blows into the cup, then tries again.)* Still too hot... *(Gets up and carries the cup to the sink, where he turns on the faucet and puts cold water in the cup. It overflows, so he turns off the faucet, returns to the table and sits. He sips the coffee slowly.)* Needs sugar... The coffee needs sugar... *(Gets up and looks around the kitchen for the sugar bowl.)* Where's the sugar? *(After opening a few cabinets, he sees the sugar bowl high up on a shelf. He tries to reach it, but it is too high. He pulls a chair over, stands on it unsteadily, and grabs the sugar bowl. He gets off the chair, sits down at the table, and puts three spoonfuls of sugar in the coffee. He sips it again.)* Needs more sugar... The coffee needs more sugar... *(Puts three more spoonfuls of sugar in the cup, then sips it again.)* Needs more sugar... *(Puts three more spoonfuls in the cup, then hears voices at the apartment door. He gets up, puts the sugar bowl on the counter, and EXITS RIGHT with the coffee cup.)*

ESTELLE: *(From OFF LEFT.)* Come on in for a minute, Martha.

MARTHA: *(From OFF LEFT.)* I've got to get dinner on the table. *(The door opens, and ESTELLE ENTERS LEFT. She wears a simple dress and hat and carries a purse. MARTHA ENTERS behind her and is dressed similarly.)*

ESTELLE: Leo can wait a few minutes.

MARTHA: It was such an exhausting day at work, wasn't it?

ESTELLE: Business is booming. I must have sold ten toasters just this afternoon.

MARTHA: I don't even know how many pots and pans I sold.

ESTELLE: Come in. I've got to show you what I found for Suzanne.

MARTHA: Well, just for a minute.

ESTELLE: *(Calls OFF RIGHT.)* Suzanne! Are you home? *(No response.)* She's out, so it's safe to show you. You've got to see this! *(Takes off her hat as she EXITS RIGHT. From OFF RIGHT.)*

I was pricing a party dress for Suzanne in several stores, but they were so expensive, even if you have enough ration coupons. *(ENTERS RIGHT without her hat and purse, but now carrying a girl's pink dress.)* Then look what I found in a re-sale shop on Bronxdale Avenue!

MARTHA: It's darling!

ESTELLE: I might have to take it in a little, but not much.

MARTHA: Suzanne will love it, I'm sure.

ESTELLE: There's a tiny little stain right here. *(Points it out.)* But I can get rid of that.

MARTHA: A little Ivory soap ought to do it.

ESTELLE: *(EXITS RIGHT. From OFF RIGHT.)* I better hide it in case she walks in. I want it to be a surprise for her birthday tomorrow. *(Calls.)* Wilbur! Wilbur! Are you home, Wilbur? *(ENTERS RIGHT.)* Ten years old! Can you believe my little girl is going to be ten?

MARTHA: Such a sweet age! *(WILBUR ENTERS RIGHT, but stays in the doorway.)*

ESTELLE: Wilbur! You are home.

MARTHA: Hello, Wilbur…

WILBUR: *(Nervous.)* Hello…

ESTELLE: Where's Suzanne?

WILBUR: I… I… don't know…

ESTELLE: You don't know? Didn't she come home from school?

WILBUR: School? Oh, yes, she came home… from school…

ESTELLE: Then what?

WILBUR: She… came home from school…

ESTELLE: Yes? Yes?

WILBUR: Then… she went out again.

ESTELLE: Where did she go?

WILBUR: I… I don't know.

ESTELLE: Wilbur! You're her father. Why didn't you ask where she was going?

WILBUR: She… she said…

ESTELLE: Yes? What did she say?

WILBUR: She said… she was going to… Caroline's house… to play.

ESTELLE: Caroline? Are you sure she didn't say Carolann? I don't think Suzanne even knows a Caroline.

WILBUR: Maybe it was Carolann... I forget.

ESTELLE: That's okay, Wilbur. So she's at Carolann's. Fine.

WILBUR: *(Starts to EXIT, slowly.)* I thought she said Caroline... I forget... *(EXITS RIGHT.)*

MARTHA: Poor Wilbur. He doesn't seem to be any better.

ESTELLE: Those people at the hospital said he was well enough to go home. I wonder if they were right.

MARTHA: I didn't know they released patients from a mental hospital.

ESTELLE: Well, they released this one. Five years he was in there. They had to do some of those electric shocks, you know. To calm him down.

MARTHA: Do you think it helped?

ESTELLE: Well, he sure is calm. Too calm. And he says he can't taste food. I guess his taste buds got shocked out of him.

MARTHA: I've got to get going to—

ESTELLE: Oh! One other thing! Guess what other surprise I have for Suzanne's birthday? I'm making a cake!

MARTHA: A cake! How did you find the ingredients?

ESTELLE: After getting through the Depression standing in bread and soup lines just to eat anything, I figured I can make it work with the rationing now.

MARTHA: I suppose needing coupons to get food isn't as bad as when we were starving. But still!

ESTELLE: I've been hoarding my eggs. Wilbur doesn't care what he eats for breakfast. I usually give him toast with a little oil on it. I have just enough cooking oil. And I finally saved up enough sugar!

MARTHA: Sugar! How did you manage?

ESTELLE: I've been saving up sugar ration coupons for weeks. *(Pulls a chair to the cabinet and stands on it.)* I hid the sugar bowl up here so Wilbur couldn't—*(Looks inside the cabinet.)* It's gone! The sugar bowl is gone!

MARTHA: *(Sees the bowl on the counter.)* Here it is, Estelle! Right on the counter.

ESTELLE: Thank goodness. *(Climbs down from the chair.)* For a moment I thought—

MARTHA: But it's nearly empty. *(Hands her the bowl.)*

ESTELLE: Empty? I had just over a cup of sugar in here—*(Realizes.)* Wilbur! *(Shouts.)* Wilbur! Come in here!

MARTHA: Oh, dear.

ESTELLE: Did you hear me, Wilbur? Come in here!

MARTHA: Maybe I better go.

WILBUR: *(APPEARS in the doorway, innocent.)* Yes, Estelle...?

MARTHA: *(Stern.)* What happened to my sugar?

WILBUR: I... I... I forget.

MARTHA: *(Angry.)* You forgot! Did you also forget that tomorrow is your daughter's birthday? I was saving that sugar to make her a birthday cake!

WILBUR: *(Confused.)* Birthday cake?

MARTHA: Yes! I need one full cup of sugar to make the cake. *(Shows him the sugar bowl.)* And this is all that's left!

WILBUR: I... I... remember. Coffee. I had some coffee...

ESTELLE: A whole bowl of sugar for a cup of coffee?

WILBUR: I had some coffee...

ESTELLE: *(Disgusted.)* Oh, Wilbur!

WILBUR: I still have some left.

ESTELLE: Sugar?

WILBUR: Coffee. I... I better go finish it. *(EXITS RIGHT, slowly.)*

ESTELLE: *(To MARTHA.)* Now what am I going to do? The recipe calls for a full cup of sugar.

MARTHA: I'd give you any sugar I had, Estelle. But we've been out of sugar for over a week. Leo begged me to bake some cookies last week, and I couldn't say no.

ESTELLE: It's kind of you to offer, Martha. I appreciate it. But what am I going to do?

MARTHA: Who would have any sugar that you could buy?

ESTELLE: Old Mrs. Higgins!

MARTHA: Mrs. Higgins?

ESTELLE: She's just down the hall.

MARTHA: The old woman who can't see very good?

ESTELLE: She's diabetic, but she gets sugar rations just the same. I'll bet she has some sugar she's willing to sell. *(Crosses LEFT.)* I'll just go down and knock on her door.

MARTHA: You better knock loud. She's also a little deaf.

ESTELLE: *(Stops at the door.)* Oh, Martha. Can you do me a favor?

MARTHA: I think so.

ESTELLE: Stay here until I get back.

MARTHA: Why?

ESTELLE: So that Wilbur doesn't get to my eggs and my cooking oil. Where's my purse? *(Rushes OFF RIGHT.)*

MARTHA: Well...

ESTELLE: *(From OFF RIGHT.)* I'll be right back. *(RE-ENTERS RIGHT with her purse.)* Please?

MARTHA: Okay.

ESTELLE: You're a dear! Wish me luck! *(EXITS LEFT. MARTHA goes to the table and sits. In a moment, WILBUR ENTERS RIGHT.)*

WILBUR: Estelle?

MARTHA: *(Rises, nervous.)* Wilbur!

WILBUR: Estelle, I'm sorry about the sugar.

MARTHA: Estelle just went out for a moment. She'll be right back.

WILBUR: *(Confused.)* You're not Estelle...

MARTHA: That's right, Wilbur. I'm Martha, from next door. Estelle will be here in a few minutes.

WILBUR: I'm sorry about the sugar.

MARTHA: I'm sure you are, Wilbur. *(The front door opens, and SUZANNE ENTERS LEFT. She is dressed in a plain, somewhat faded dress and has a ribbon in her hair.)*

SUZANNE: Mom! *(Sees MARTHA.)* Oh, hello, Mrs. Farley. Hi, Dad.

MARTHA: Happy birthday one day early, Suzanne!

SUZANNE: Thanks! *(To WILBUR.)* Where's Mom?

WILBUR: I... I forget...

MARTHA: She's just down the hall at Mrs. Higgins's apartment. She'll be right back.

SUZANNE: Mrs. Higgins? The old lady?

MARTHA: That's the one.

SUZANNE: *(To WILBUR.)* What's she doing there?

WILBUR: I... I forget...

MARTHA: She'll be back any moment.

WILBUR: *(To SUZANNE.)* You were at Caroline's house.

SUZANNE: Carolann, Dad. I don't know any Caroline.

WILBUR: Oh... *(The door opens, and ESTELLE ENTERS LEFT triumphantly with a sugar bowl.)*

ESTELLE: Success!

MARTHA: You did it!

SUZANNE: Did what?

ESTELLE: Suzanne, you're home! Guess what we're gonna do together tonight!

SUZANNE: What?

ESTELLE: We are gonna make a birthday cake!

SUZANNE: Really?

ESTELLE: We certainly are! *(Holds up the sugar bowl.)* I've got the sugar right here!

MARTHA: That's wonderful!

WILBUR: Sugar?

ESTELLE: A birthday cake for my ten-year-old girl!

SUZANNE: *(Excited.)* Hooray!

WILBUR: Estelle...?

ESTELLE: What is it, Wilbur?

WILBUR: I'm sorry about the sugar. *(BLACKOUT.)*

AFTERMATH

One of the greatest ills of the rationing system was the black market, where one could illegally buy rationed items at high prices. The most sought after products on the black market were meat, gasoline, and sugar. Although World War II ended in 1945, shortages continued for a time, and the rationing program was not discontinued until 1946.

VJ DAY BLUES
(1945)

BACKGROUND

During World War II, many factories that manufactured domestic items, like refrigerators and cars, received government contracts to make jeeps, military arms, and other items needed for the war effort. With so many American men serving overseas, these businesses for the first time hired women for factory work. The nickname "Rosie the Riveter" was applied to these thousands of female employees doing what was previously considered men's work. Many black men were also hired for jobs that were once only given to white men. All this changed when World War II ended.

SETTING

TIME: August 16, 1945—the day after VJ Day (Victory Over Japan Day).

PLACE: The employee coatroom in the factory for Wellsford Company in Lowell, Massachusetts.

CHARACTERS

KITTY (F) .... female factory worker
ELLIE (F) .... older female factory worker
DOREEN (F) .... another
RITA (F) .... another
MR. JENKINS (M) .... foreman
CARL (M) .... black man

SET DESCRIPTION

The door to the coatroom is RIGHT. A bank of lockers and coat hooks line the walls. There are also a few benches and wartime posters that say, "Loose Lips Sink Ships" and "Buy War Bonds."

PROPERTIES

Mop, bucket of water (CARL).

LIGHTS UP on the empty coatroom. ELLIE and KITTY ENTER RIGHT in mid-conversation. Each wears a one-piece jumpsuit and a headscarf.

KITTY: What a party! It must have been after one o'clock before I got home!

ELLIE: At your age, I could stay out late and still show up for work on time. Not anymore.

KITTY: Didn't you celebrate at all? After all, yesterday was VJ Day!

ELLIE: I listened to the radio and heard plenty of celebrating. But all I kept thinking was, "Jack's coming home! Jack's coming home!"

KITTY: Ellie, you must be so relieved!

ELLIE: Last I knew, he was in the Philippines. Of course I am relieved! I'm deliriously relieved!

KITTY: *(Not enthusiastic.)* I suppose Myron will be coming home, too.

ELLIE: Are you still stringing him along?

KITTY: I didn't want to write him a Dear John letter. They say it's bad for military morale.

ELLIE: Now you'll have to tell him face-to-face.

KITTY: Maybe he's forgotten all about me. I hardly ever wrote him.

ELLIE: He'll remember you. *(DOREEN and RITA ENTER RIGHT, dressed in the same outfits.)*

DOREEN: *(To KITTY.)* Look who's early for once! Kitty, I figured you'd be out celebrating all night.

ELLIE: She practically was.

KITTY: I wasn't going to be late today. I'm not giving Mr. Jenkins a reason to fire me. I love this job.

RITA: We all do. Why do you think Doreen and I are early as well?

DOREEN: Early or late, I think our days here are numbered.

KITTY: Don't say such a thing!

DOREEN: The war's over. Things are going to change.

RITA: I've been here three years, and I figured out that I've helped make over three thousand propellers. Doesn't that count for anything?

ELLIE: Rita, I don't think there will be such a demand for airplane propellers now.

KITTY: But I thought that Wellsford Company would go back to making auto hubcaps again. Like before the war.

DOREEN: I think they're going to go after bigger fish than hubcaps.

RITA: Like what, Doreen?

DOREEN: It's just a rumor, but I heard they're going to completely redo the factory and make air conditioners for cars.

KITTY: That's ridiculous! Who wants air conditioning in their car?

ELLIE: *(Laughs.)* Not while we still got "four and sixty."

KITTY: What's "four and sixty"?

DOREEN/ELLIE/RITA: *(Chant together.)* "All four windows down at sixty miles an hour!" *(ALL laugh.)*

KITTY: Air conditioning in cars! What a stupid idea.

ELLIE: It's the future.

RITA: Well, hubcaps or air conditioning, I still want to work here. We sure need the money at home.

DOREEN: I made more money working here than Harold ever did pumping gas. It's a good thing he ain't alive to see it. He'd have a fit!

KITTY: Ellie, do you think Jack will want you to continue working?

ELLIE: I don't know. I'll be so happy to have him back that I'll stay home and make cookies all day if he wants!

DOREEN: Maybe there will be enough sugar again to make cookies.

RITA: And birthday cakes for my kids!

KITTY: And nylons! Real and actual nylons!

ELLIE: Yes, a lot of things will get better with the war over.

DOREEN: I hope I never see another ration coupon in my life!

KITTY: I want to buy a car! Now there will be plenty of gasoline!

RITA: Your car going to have air conditioning in it? *(ALL laugh.)*

KITTY: Laugh all you want! But this lousy war is finally over, and I'm going to start living!

ELLIE: It costs money to "start living," Kitty.

KITTY: *(Proud.)* I am an independent working girl!

DOREEN: Was.

KITTY: If I can't work here, I'll get another job.

RITA: Sure you will. Slinging hash down at Tillerman's Diner.

DOREEN: Or making beds at the Twin Oaks Motel.

ELLIE: Now, let's not be so negative, girls. We don't know yet what the future brings.

KITTY: That's telling them, Ellie. It's going to be a new world. Especially for women!

DOREEN: *(Sarcastic.)* So women are going to take over? Oh, that's real nice.

ELLIE: Consider this. This country wouldn't have won this war without all of us Rosie the Riveters.

RITA: That's true.

DOREEN: Somebody gonna tell the men that?

ELLIE: *(Looks OFF RIGHT.)* Uh-oh...

RITA: It's Mr. Jenkins. Kitty, why don't you tell him about this whole new world for women?

KITTY: Shush, Rita! *(Towards door RIGHT.)* Good morning, Mr. Jenkins!

MR. JENKINS: *(ENTERS RIGHT, walking with a slight limp. He seems older than his years. He wears faded trousers, a white shirt, and a bow tie.)* Not so sure about that. You ladies are here pretty early today.

RITA: The war may be over, but a job still has to be done.

MR. JENKINS: Not so sure about that.

ELLIE: Any word about your grandson, Mr. Jenkins?

MR. JENKINS: No, sorry to say. Still missing in action. With the surrender, maybe we'll finally learn the truth.

ELLIE: I hope you get good news real soon.

MR. JENKINS: Hope so, too. Well, the government won't need any more propellers from us, that's for certain. I got a call from Mr. Wellsford last night. We're to close down the line.

DOREEN: Today?

MR. JENKINS: No use making something nobody wants.

RITA: Someone must need airplane propellers.

MR. JENKINS: Not the government. Not anymore.

ELLIE: What about us, Mr. Jenkins?

MR. JENKINS: No use hanging around here. There's no more work.

KITTY: None for now. But later?

MR. JENKINS: Don't know about that. They don't tell me a thing.

DOREEN: But you're the foreman!

MR. JENKINS: Was. With all the young fellas coming home, who wants a sixty-six-year-old foreman?

RITA: Then we're all fired?

MR. JENKINS: Let's just say that we're all "retired."

KITTY: I'm only twenty-eight!

MR. JENKINS: Call it early retirement then. It'll take the girls in the office a few days to type up your... retirement letters. And you'll each get a paycheck for two extra weeks. That's 'cause the company couldn't give you two weeks' notice. It'll probably take a week, but those checks are coming. Oh, and you can keep your work clothes. Most of them are too small for men anyway. I think that's about everything. I better get out to the gate so I can tell the others as they arrive. Any questions? Though I doubt I can answer them.

DOREEN: Will Wellsford go back to making hubcaps?

MR. JENKINS: Darned if I know.

DOREEN: I heard they're going to go into air conditioning for cars. Any truth in that?

MR. JENKINS: Air conditioning? For cars? *(Chuckles.)* That's a good one! *(Laughs a bit more.)* Yes, that is a good one. First laugh I've had in months... *(As he EXITS.)* Cars with air conditioning... What will they think of next?! *(EXITS RIGHT. A long silence.)*

KITTY: *(Angry.)* It's not fair!

DOREEN: They used us when they needed us. Now they don't need us.

ELLIE: Well, it was nice while it lasted.

RITA: I'll never forget it. I was proud of being a Rosie the Riveter.

ELLIE: I think we all were.

KITTY: We did men's work!

DOREEN: 'Cause the men were all gone. Now they're coming back.

RITA: And we go back to being just... just...

KITTY: Women.

DOREEN: No use sticking around here any longer. Rita, let's go.

RITA: My kids are sure gonna be surprised to see me walk through that door.

DOREEN: Goodbye, ladies. See you around town.

ELLIE: I'm sure we will. Bye, Doreen. Bye, Rita.

DOREEN: *(To RITA as they both head RIGHT.)* My kids have been running wild all summer. Can't wait for school to start in a few weeks. *(They EXIT RIGHT.)*

KITTY: I still say it's not fair!

ELLIE: I know, Kitty. Especially for you. You're young. You thought you had a career.

KITTY: Now what do I have? Nothing!

ELLIE: You have a future. Not here, but somewhere. It's your generation that will change things.

KITTY: I hope you're right, Ellie. 'Cause I sure as heck don't want to marry Myron and settle down so the rest of my life is just having kids and making cookies!

ELLIE: *(Smiles.)* No, that's not the life for you, Kitty.

KITTY: Goodbye, Ellie.

ELLIE: Lowell is a small city. We'll run into each other. Until then... bye. *(KITTY EXITS RIGHT, and ELLIE sits on a bench, emotionally exhausted. In a moment, CARL ENTERS RIGHT. He also wears a one-piece jumpsuit, and he carries a mop and a bucket of water. He stops when he sees ELLIE.)*

CARL: I thought everybody was gone.

ELLIE: Everybody but me. *(Rises.)* I was just leaving.

CARL: Mr. Jenkins said I should mop up once everyone was gone.

ELLIE: Mop up? What for?

CARL: Durned if I know.

ELLIE: I recognize you... *(Tries to think of his name.)* Cal?

CARL: Carl.

ELLIE: Carl! You drive one of the trucks.

CARL: Not no more.

ELLIE: Were you also... "retired"?

CARL: Mr. Jenkins say I can have my old job back. Afore the war, I mopped up every night. Then when all the white boys was gone, they made me a driver. For four years I drove them trucks. Now the war being over, I go back to mopping.

ELLIE: But the factory is shut down.

CARL: Open or closed, no matter what they make, there's always someone who's got to mop up. And I guess that's me.

ELLIE: I see... *(Starts to leave, then stops.)* I'll bet you were a heck of a truck driver, Carl.

CARL: *(Proud.)* I was, ma'am. I sure was. *(ELLIE smiles, then EXITS RIGHT as CARL starts to mop the floor. LIGHTS SLOWLY FADE OUT.)*

AFTERMATH

Many of the women employed in factories during World War II wanted to continue their jobs, though some wished to return to being housewives and others hoped to get married and start families. Over two million women working in factories were let go once the servicemen returned. Of the women who did continue to work, most could only find employment as waitresses, maids, secretaries, teachers, and other positions traditionally held by women before the war. Two decades would pass before the number of women in the workforce was as high as during World War II.

'TIL FURTHER NOTICE
(1951)

BACKGROUND

Poliomyelitis, commonly known as polio, can be a crippling and even fatal disease in extreme cases that has recurred throughout history. Epidemics of polio have sprung up over the centuries. A polio epidemic that began in the United States in the 1940s reached its peak in 1952, when there were 59,000 cases reported in all forty-eight states, plus Puerto Rico, Alaska, and Hawaii. Doctors and scientists could determine neither the cause nor a cure for the disease, which seemed to mostly affect children. Harvard scientists invented an "iron lung," a large metal ventilator in which a patient was enclosed for days or months to assist weakened or paralyzed breathing muscles with respiration. In the early 1950s, Americans feared polio more than an atomic war. In the hysteria, many people avoided schools, camps, restaurants, movie theatres, and other public places in hopes of not catching the disease.

SETTING

TIME: An early Saturday morning in October 1951.

PLACE: Outside the gates of the municipal swimming pool in San Bernardino, California.

CHARACTERS

DARCY (F)..................................... teenage swimmer
MOM (F).. her mother
GRANDMA (F) .... elderly woman
HOWIE (M)................................... Grandma's young grandson
MR. WALKER (M)........................ pool caretaker

SET DESCRIPTION

The gates to the bathhouse and the pool are locked UP LEFT. There are two benches and a drinking fountain along a wall UPSTAGE. A sign on the wall states: "POOL HOURS: 9 a.m. to 7 p.m."

PROPERTIES

Purse (MOM); small gym bag (DARCY); tool box containing a wrench, duct tape, and two rolled-up signs that respectively read: "Pool Closed Until Further Notice" and "Out of Order" (MR. WALKER).

FLEXIBLE CASTING NOTE

ALL roles could be played by either gender with only minor script adjustments.

LIGHTS UP on MOM and DARCY, sitting on a bench, waiting for the pool to open. It is a few minutes before nine o'clock in the morning. MOM wears a comfortable housedress and hat and carries a purse. DARCY wears shorts and a sweatshirt and carries a small gym bag.

DARCY: It's been almost a week since we've seen her here. It doesn't make sense.

MOM: Maybe her family is out of town on vacation.

DARCY: In October?

MOM: She could have a cold or something.

DARCY: I suppose, but she's pretty strong and healthy.

MOM: We could try to find her number in the phone book, if only we knew her last name.

DARCY: Laurie and I swam laps together every day for three months, but it never even dawned on me to get her last name or phone number.

MOM: She's a good swimmer, that's for sure.

DARCY: She's amazing! Much better than me.

MOM: Oh, I wouldn't say that, Darcy.

DARCY: I'm all right. But Laurie— *(HOWIE runs ON LEFT, followed by his GRANDMA. She wears a dated dress and hat. HOWIE wears swim trunks, a t-shirt, and beach shoes.)*

GRANDMA: Slow down, Howie! I know how anxious you are to go swimming, but—

HOWIE: The gates are closed! I wanna go swimming!

MOM: *(To GRANDMA.)* They ought to be open any minute now.

GRANDMA: Did you hear that, Howie? Look. The sign says nine o'clock.

HOWIE: What time is it now, Grandma?

GRANDMA: Just about nine. You'll only have to wait a few more minutes.

HOWIE: *(Sits on the other bench.)* Ah, gee!

GRANDMA: Such an impatient child you are. You have to learn to be more patient. *(Sits next to him.)*

HOWIE: That's what you said yesterday.

GRANDMA: *(To MOM.)* He would hardly eat his breakfast, he was so excited about going swimming. So we rush to get here, and it turns out the pool isn't even open yet!

MOM: Mr. Walker ought to be here any moment now. He's the pool caretaker.

GRANDMA: So you're regulars, I take it.

MOM: My daughter Darcy swims every day. She's in training. Weekends, we like to get here early before the pool gets too crowded. On school days, we come around five o'clock when most folks are having dinner.

GRANDMA: My, that is serious swimming! *(To DARCY.)* What are you training for, dear?

DARCY: Regional finals are in November.

MOM: Last year, Darcy made Regional. And she just missed going on to State.

DARCY: I'll get there this year.

GRANDMA: My! You must be an excellent swimmer.

MOM: She is.

HOWIE: What time is it now?

GRANDMA: You just hush up, Howie.

HOWIE: *(Whines.)* I'm thirsty!

GRANDMA: There's a drinking fountain right over there.

HOWIE: Okay. *(Goes to the fountain and drinks.)*

GRANDMA: *(To MOM.)* Howie's my grandson. He and my daughter are visiting from Indiana.

MOM: How nice.

GRANDMA: Such a long way to go, from Indiana to California! It took them three days by train! But my daughter needed to get away for a while. *(Whispers so HOWIE doesn't hear while he begins splashing in the fountain.)* Marital troubles. Nothing serious, I hope. *(To HOWIE.)* Howie, stop splashing the water. That's a drinking fountain. Save your splashing for the pool!

HOWIE: Ah, gee! *(Returns and sits.)*

MOM: Still no sign of Mr. Walker.

DARCY: Or of Laurie.

GRANDMA: *(To DARCY.)* You must be quite dedicated to your swimming. I think that's wonderful.

MOM: Darcy's been swimming since she could walk. Isn't that right, Darcy?

DARCY: *(Slightly embarrassed.)* Oh, Mom.

GRANDMA: All those hours and hours of swimming practice! Just like dancing. I used to take ballet lessons.

MOM: Oh?

GRANDMA: I was quite serious about it too! Took lessons for years! I might even have gone professional. But I gave it all up.

DARCY: Why?

GRANDMA: Oh, I got married and soon enough had a heap of kids. I have six grandchildren now, and another one on the way. Sissy is pregnant again. Howie's going to have another little sister or brother, aren't you, Howie?

HOWIE: Big deal.

GRANDMA: I love all my grandchildren. And my children, of course. The trouble with so many loved ones is you worry all the time. There's always something. Right now, I'm most worried about Martha's youngest, Daniel. He's got polio. Woke up one morning and couldn't move one of his legs. He could hardly walk. Now the weakness has spread to all his muscles. It's terrible.

MOM: I'm so sorry.

GRANDMA: Martha and Bill have cashed in their life insurance in order to pay the hospital bills. Daniel's even too weak to breathe on his own, so now he's in one of those iron lung things.

MOM: That's awful!

GRANDMA: Daniel's only ten, but he's a strong little fellow. Isn't he, Howie?

HOWIE: Who?

GRANDMA: Your cousin Daniel. Very strong.

HOWIE: He beat me up once!

GRANDMA: *(Laughs.)* I bet you started it!

HOWIE: Did not!

GRANDMA: *(Still laughing.)* Children! It doesn't matter what happens, they're all a blessing!

MOM: Darcy's an only child. *(Laughs.)* So she's terribly spoiled. Aren't you, Darcy?

DARCY: Very funny.

GRANDMA: *(To MOM.)* It must be quite a responsibility for you, too. Bringing your daughter to the pool every day.

DARCY: I take my driving test next week! Then I'll be able to drive here myself.

MOM: In whose car, may I ask?

DARCY: *(Irritable.)* Where is Mr. Walker? *(Gets up and crosses RIGHT, looking OFFSTAGE.)* He's late!

HOWIE: *(Runs back and forth.)* I wanna go swimming! I wanna go swimming!

GRANDMA: Howie, behave yourself.

MOM: *(Looks at her watch.)* It's five after nine. I don't understand it.

DARCY: Here's his truck now!

MOM: *(Rises.)* Finally!

GRANDMA: Did you hear that, Howie? The nice man who opens the gates is coming.

HOWIE: Yippee!

DARCY: But still no sign of Laurie. *(MR. WALKER ENTERS RIGHT. He wears overalls and carries a toolbox.)*

MOM: Mr. Walker! *(Lightly.)* We'd about given up on you!

MR. WALKER: *(To MOM and DARCY.)* I guessed you two would be waiting for me. I was kind of hoping you'd come later.

MOM: What do you mean, Mr. Walker?

MR. WALKER: Didn't want to have to tell you the bad news. Rather you just read the sign. *(Opens his toolbox.)*

DARCY: What bad news?

MOM: What sign?

MR. WALKER: The pool is closed. Instructions from the city Health Department. *(Pulls out some duct tape and a rolled up sign and takes them over to the wall.)*

GRANDMA: Closed?

MOM: For today?

MR. WALKER: 'Til further notice. That's what they told me to put on the sign. *(Unrolls the sign and tapes it to the wall. It reads, "Pool Closed Until Further Notice.")*

MOM: I don't understand. Why?

MR. WALKER: I'm not supposed to say.

HOWIE: I wanna go swimming!

GRANDMA: *(To MR. WALKER.)* It's because of polio, isn't it?

MR. WALKER: You didn't hear it from me, but, yes, ma'am, it's because of polio. All the public pools in the county are shutting down. Those at the YMCA and YWCA, too.

MOM: It's in the water?

GRANDMA: They say it spreads to other children in the water.

MR. WALKER: That's what they think. Better to be safe than sorry.

HOWIE: I wanna go swimming!

MR. WALKER: Take the kid to the ocean. No threat in salt water, they say. *(Brings his toolbox over to the drinking fountain and kneels on the ground. Pulls out a wrench.)*

HOWIE: The ocean! I wanna swim in the ocean! I wanna swim in the ocean!

GRANDMA: Okay, Howie. Get back in the car.

HOWIE: The ocean! *(Starts running.)* I'm gonna swim in the ocean! *(Runs OFF LEFT.)*

GRANDMA: *(To DARCY.)* I'm so sorry, dear, but you'll find someplace else to practice your swimming.

MOM: Where?

GRANDMA: I don't know... somewhere. *(Smiles, encouragingly.)* After all, you're going to State, remember?

HOWIE: *(From OFF LEFT.)* Grandma, come on!

GRANDMA: Now I have to drive all the way to the ocean! *(Smiles.)* Children! *(EXITS LEFT.)*

MR. WALKER: *(To MOM and DARCY.)* So sorry, ladies. I know how hard the young one here has been practicing.

MOM: We'll find somewhere else.

MR. WALKER: Just be sure it ain't a public pool. *(Finishes working on the drinking fountain and tapes another sign to it that reads: "Out of Order.")*

MOM: The drinking fountains, too?

MR. WALKER: Them are my orders. Better—

MOM: Better safe than sorry. I know. Come on home, Darcy. We'll figure something out.

DARCY: Mr. Walker? You're here most of the time, right?

MR. WALKER: Not any more.

DARCY: But in the last week, have you seen Laurie come to the pool?

MOM: She's the girl that practices with Darcy sometimes.

MR. WALKER: The red-haired girl?

DARCY: Yes! That's her.

MR. WALKER: Her mother came by the other day to get something her daughter left in the bathhouse. Goggles, I think it was. *(Closes up the toolbox.)*

DARCY: But not Laurie?

MR. WALKER: No. Her mother said the girl was sick... with polio. It seems to be everywhere these days. *(EXITS RIGHT with his toolbox. DARCY and MOM embrace. LIGHTS SLOWLY FADE OUT.)*

AFTERMATH

To this day, it is not known exactly how polio spreads, and most of the precautions in the 1950s were useless. Although Dr. Jonas Salk first developed a polio vaccine in 1948, and it was improved upon by Albert Sabin in 1950, it took years of testing and study before the polio vaccine was widely used in 1954. By 1964, because of the increased awareness of the polio vaccine through the March of Dimes program, there were only 121 reported cases of polio in the United States. All the same, today there are still thousands of Americans who are partially or totally crippled or paralyzed from the epidemic of the 1950s.

Dr. Salk chose not to patent the polio vaccine, which accelerated its availability internationally. By the 1990s, the world was almost totally free of polio. Since the beginning of the 21st century, however, some parents have refused to have their children vaccinated, and measles, pertussis, and mumps are already beginning to re-appear in alarming numbers. Without a one-hundred-percent vaccination rate, it is only a matter of time before polio also returns to America.

WAITING FOR THE BUS

(1955)

BACKGROUND

Among the Jim Crow laws and segregation statutes still enforced in the South in the 1950s were separate restrooms, drinking fountains, and bus seating for white and black citizens. In Montgomery, Alabama, blacks were required to sit in the "colored section" of city buses and to give up their seats to white passengers, if needed. In 1943, Rosa Parks became a member of the National Association for the Advancement of Colored People (NAACP), and by 1955, she was the secretary for the Montgomery chapter. She also worked as a seamstress at a downtown department store. Her husband, Raymond Parks, was also a member of the NAACP, and he worked as a barber.

SETTING

TIME: Around 5:30 p.m. on December 1, 1955.

PLACE: A bus stop in downtown Montgomery, Alabama.

CHARACTERS

REEVA (F) .... middle-aged black seamstress
BELINDA (F) .... another
ROSA PARKS (F) .... another
ETTA (F) .... black store clerk

SET DESCRIPTION

There is a sign indicating the bus stop and a trash can nearby.

PROPERTIES

Purse (REEVA, BELINDA, ROSA, ETTA); paper shopping bag containing a large black and white striped dress wrapped in tissue paper (REEVA).

SOUND EFFECTS

Rush hour traffic, bus going by, bus approaching, bus stopping, bus door opening.

SOUND EFFECT: RUSH HOUR TRAFFIC continues throughout the scene. LIGHTS UP on REEVA, BELINDA, and ROSA standing together talking at a bus stop. ETTA also stands at the bus stop. It is cold, and all four WOMEN wear simple but presentable coats and hats, and each carries a purse. REEVA also carries a paper shopping bag.

REEVA: I knew when I was doing her measurements last week that no way was that fat woman going to look good in that dress.

BELINDA: Not fat, Reeva. The customer is never fat.

ROSA: Pleasantly plump.

BELINDA: No. Full-figured! *(ALL laugh.)*

REEVA: Call it what you want, this lady was wide as a house. And the dress was all stripes and such. I thought I was measuring a pregnant zebra! *(ALL laugh.)*

ROSA: So what happened when she tried it on today?

REEVA: What do you think? She looked at herself in the mirror and just about had her a stroke! "This is not the dress I tried on last week," she says. "It can't be!" Mrs. Keller, she looks at the ticket and says real polite like, "Oh, yes, ma'am. The black and white cocktail dress." Then the pleasantly plump lady—

BELINDA: You mean, full-figured!

REEVA: I mean fat! She gets all huffy and says, "Well, there's something wrong with the alterations!" So Mrs. Keller, she calls me over and says, "Reeva, did your do these alterations correctly?" And I says, "Yes, ma'am. I took the measurements myself and altered the dress just like I wrote it down."

BELINDA: Mrs. Keller thinks you don't know how to measure? You been at Dunnigan's for twenty years!

ROSA: Mrs. Keller thinks no one knows as much as Mrs. Keller.

BELINDA: *(To REEVA.)* What happened then?

REEVA: Well, the white lady gets all huffy again and says, "I'm not paying for this dress! It's a disgrace! If Dunnigan's cannot do something as simple as alterations, then I'll take my business elsewhere!"

ROSA: Uh-oh...

BELINDA: Those words are the kiss of death to Mrs. Keller. I'll bet she got all red in the face.

REEVA: She did, but before she could get a word out, the fat lady went into the dressing room, and Mrs. Keller took it out on me. "Reeva, you have ruined this dress!"

BELINDA: What?!

REEVA: "I ain't ruined nothin'!" I says. "That is a perfectly good dress. It just don't look good on her. I can alter any dress, but I can't alter them that wears it!"

ROSA: Good girl!

BELINDA: I hope the fat lady heard you.

REEVA: That was what Mrs. Keller was afraid of. She whispers to me real loud, "Shush your mouth, Reeva!" And before you know it, the fat lady comes out of the dressing room, carrying the dress. I couldn't believe such a... full-figured gal could get out of one dress and into another one so fast! *(ALL laugh.)*

BELINDA: What happened then? Tell us before my bus comes!

REEVA: Well, the fat lady don't say a word. She tosses the dress to Mrs. Keller and marches herself over to the escalator and goes down. But Mrs. Keller is still red in the face, and she says to me, "Reeva, you have ruined this dress, and the cost will be deducted from your paycheck!"

BELINDA: What?!

ROSA: She can't do that!

REEVA: I didn't know what to say at first, I was so surprised. It was a sixty-dollar dress!

BELINDA: Sixty dollars! No dress at Dunnigan's is worth that much!

REEVA: Then an idea comes to me. I says to Mrs. Keller, "If you are gonna take the money out of my pay, I want the dress!"

BELINDA: Makes sense.

REEVA: Mrs. Keller, she says, "The dress is ruined. It goes in the scrap barrel." I says, "There ain't nothing wrong with that dress. If I gotta pay for it, I want it!"

ROSA: What did she say to that?

REEVA: The same fool thing she always says. "I'll have to check with Mr. Henley about that."

BELINDA: That sure sounds just like her.

ROSA: If that store caught on fire, she'd check with Mr. Henley before she jumped out the window! *(ALL laugh.)*

BELINDA: So you got the dress?

REEVA: Sure did! Mrs. Keller comes to me right before I clock out and says I can have the dress, but Mr. Henley says no employee discount. And here it is! *(Holds up the shopping bag and shakes* *it.)* It's gonna cost me sixty bucks, but I got it! *(Laughs.)* First dress I ever got without having to hound Alfred!

ROSA: Will it fit you?

REEVA: It sure will, once I alter it again. There's enough material on this zebra skin to make two dresses! *(ALL laugh.)*

ETTA: Can I see it?

REEVA: *(Surprised to hear from ETTA.)* What's that?

ETTA: Can I please see it, ma'am?

REEVA: Sure can, honey. *(Puts the bag down and goes through the tissue paper.)*

BELINDA: I seen you at Dunnigan's. The makeup counter?

ETTA: Perfume.

ROSA: They ain't gonna let no colored girl try to sell makeup to white women.

REEVA: Here she is! *(Holds up a black and white striped dress.)*

BELINDA: My, that's something!

REEVA: For sixty dollars, it better be!

ROSA: You wear that to church on Sunday, and folks will think you been to Paris!

REEVA: Paris, Texas! *(ALL laugh.)* I better not tell Alfred until I can come up with a good story. *(Puts the dress away.)*

ETTA: It's a very pretty dress, ma'am.

REEVA: Call me Reeva.

ETTA: I'm Etta.

ROSA: Did you know, ladies, that Etta is the first colored girl to work at a first floor counter at Dunnigan's?

BELINDA: Hallelujah! *(To ETTA.)* I'm Belinda. Glad to meet you.

REEVA: Why, you're so young and pretty, Etta, I think that's right where you should be!

ROSA: Not in the back rooms like us seamstresses.

ETTA: Some of the ladies seem a little hesitant about asking me for help. Especially if there is a white girl with me.

REEVA: They'll get used to the idea. Especially if you smell all perfumey.

BELINDA: Let me have a sniff. *(Sniffs ETTA'S ear.)* Ohhh! That is heavenly stuff!

ROSA: They make you pay for the perfume you wear?

ETTA: I can spray some on at the store, but I can't take any home.

REEVA: Be sure you don't break a bottle, or you'll end up like me. A sixty-dollar dress! *(ALL laugh.)*

BELINDA: Here comes a bus!

REEVA: Is it the Summit Avenue?

BELINDA: Can't tell... *(SOUND EFFECT: BUS GOING BY.)* No. It was the express.

ROSA: You like your job, Etta?

ETTA: I sure do, but it doesn't pay much. And I had to buy some dress-up clothes to wear to work. I think my first three paychecks all went for dresses and shoes.

BELINDA: Maybe you should have bought yourself a heavier coat while you were at it. You must be freezing in that light thing you're wearing.

ETTA: I don't mind the cold.

REEVA: Winter is here. It's December already. I swear the colder it gets, the later my bus seems to come.

ROSA: Which bus are you waiting for, Etta?

ETTA: The Clinton crosstown.

BELINDA: You live in Clinton Pines?

ETTA: No. I take it to the end of the line, then I gotta walk two miles home.

REEVA: That's a lot of walking in this cold.

ROSA: I gotta take two buses, but it gets me close to home.

BELINDA: You gotta transfer at Walnut Street?

ROSA: No. Cleveland Avenue. Sometimes I wait for each bus so long, it takes me near an hour to get home. They need to have more buses that go from downtown to the colored neighborhoods.

REEVA: What I hate is when the colored section of the bus is full, and I gotta stand all the way home.

ROSA: Raymond says there oughtn't be no colored section.

BELINDA: *(To ETTA.)* Rosa's husband is a member of the NAACP.

ROSA: So am I.

BELINDA: Real radicals, both of them.

ROSA: I ain't a radical. Neither is Raymond. Is Dr. Martin Luther King a radical?

ETTA: Who?

BELINDA: I'm just saying you like to stir up trouble sometimes.

ROSA: Because I ask Mr. Henley why there ain't ever enough toilet paper in the colored's bathroom?

REEVA: Now that is radical!

BELINDA: I just mean you are the type that keeps asking questions of the white folks. "Why can't a colored family live in Clinton Pines? How come the white janitor makes more per hour than the black janitor?" Things like that.

ROSA: Those are questions that have to be asked.

BELINDA: And now you're talking about no colored section in the back of the bus!

ROSA: That's right. Raymond says the bus company depends on colored folks.

REEVA: What?

ROSA: It's true. Seventy-five percent of the bus riders in Montgomery are colored people. If we all boycott the buses, the company will lose lots of money. That'll force them to change.

ETTA: How will we get to work?

BELINDA: Yeah! Answer that, Miss NAACP!

ROSA: The NAACP will organize special shuttle buses. Other people can carpool or even walk. The colored taxi drivers have said they'd help out, too.

REEVA: I don't know. It sounds kinda—

BELINDA: Radical!

REEVA: Here comes a bus. I hope it's mine. *(SOUND EFFECT: BUS APPROACHING.)*

ROSA: Sorry, Reeva. It's the Cleveland Avenue. Goodbye, ladies. See you tomorrow.

BELINDA: *(Sarcastic.)* Wouldn't you rather wait for an NAACP shuttle?

ROSA: I've waited enough. I just want to sit down and get off these tired feet. *(SOUND EFFECT: BUS STOPPING and the DOOR OPENING. BLACKOUT.)*

AFTERMATH

Rosa Parks took a seat in the colored section of the bus, but as the bus got more crowded, the conductor told her to give her seat to a white passenger and stand instead. She refused, the police were called, and Parks was arrested for "civil disobedience." The arrest led to a public outcry and a boycott of city buses by blacks. The boycott lasted 15 months before the Supreme Court ruled that segregation on public buses was unconstitutional. Considered the first mass protest against segregation in America, Rosa Parks's court case and the boycott received national attention and was one of the most influential events in the growing civil rights movement.

ABOUT THE SIZE
OF A BEACH BALL
(1957)

BACKGROUND

After years of secret research and development, the Soviet Union launched its first satellite, *Sputnik 1*, on October 4, 1957. It was the first man-made object to penetrate space and orbit Earth. It traveled eighteen thousand miles per hour, completely orbiting Earth once every 96.2 minutes, while sending radio messages every few seconds. The satellite was visible to the naked eye as it circled Earth, and radio operators around the globe were able to pick up its Russian messages, which were about conditions in the ionosphere, such as air density and temperature. With the Cold War raging, Americans were both fascinated and frightened by the Russian achievement that introduced the Space Age.

SETTING

TIME: Twilight on October 5, 1957.
PLACE: The backyard patio of a home in suburban Oklahoma City.

CHARACTERS

AGATHA (F) .... eight-year-old girl
GRANDPA (M) .... Agatha's grandfather; retired teacher
MYRA (F) .... Agatha and Susan's mom; Grandpa's daughter
SUSAN (F) .... Agatha's older sister

SET DESCRIPTION

The patio is furnished with lawn chairs, a metal barbecue grill, and potted flowers. There is a back door to the house that leads to the kitchen UP LEFT.

PROPERTIES

Men's brown sweater (AGATHA); textbook, dish towel (SUSAN).

FLEXIBLE CASTING NOTE

AGATHA and SUSAN can be played by either gender with only minor script adjustments.

LIGHTS UP on the patio of a modest suburban home. AGATHA bursts IN through the door and looks up at the sky, excited. She is eight years old and wears a dress, a sweater, and ribbons in her hair.

AGATHA: *(Calls OFF LEFT.)* Grandpa! Hurry up, Grandpa! We're going to miss it!

GRANDPA: *(Slowly ENTERS through the door LEFT. He wears gray trousers, a white shirt, and a tie.)* Hold your horses, Agatha. The Oklahoma City *Record* said it wouldn't be visible in our neck of the woods until seven o'clock.

AGATHA: But what if it's early?

GRANDPA: *(Laughs.)* I don't think a satellite can be early. It moves at the same speed all the time. Just like a planet or a moon.

AGATHA: Mama says it's coming over here to spy on us. Is that true, Grandpa? Are the Russians spying on us?

GRANDPA: I'm sure they are, but not with Sputnik. It can't see anything or take photos. It just sends messages back to Earth about atmospheric pressure and air density and such.

AGATHA: How come I can't understand you when you talk science? You're not a teacher anymore, you know.

GRANDPA: Not for a long time, Agatha. But it's hard to give up science. What don't you understand?

AGATHA: Well... why is it called Sputnik? That's an awful silly name.

GRANDPA: It does sound a little silly to us. But in Russian, "sputnik" is the word for satellite. They decided to just call it "satellite." Sputnik.

AGATHA: That wasn't very imaginative, was it?

GRANDPA: *(Laughs.)* I suppose not!

MYRA: *(ENTERS from the kitchen wearing a housedress and an apron.)* Dad! You'll catch your death of a cold out here without a sweater. Agatha, run inside and get Grandpa's thick sweater. The brown one with the zipper.

AGATHA: Okay, Mom. *(Starts for the door.)*

GRANDPA: It's hanging on the doorknob in my bedroom.

MYRA: *(To AGATHA.)* And you change into your yellow sweater. It's too chilly out here for that one.

AGATHA: I hate that yellow sweater!

MYRA: No one is going to see it out here in the dark. Go!

AGATHA: Okay... *(EXITS LEFT.)*

GRANDPA: She's quite excited about seeing Sputnik. It's a clear night, so we ought to get a good view of it.

MYRA: *(Sarcastic.)* Pardon my lack of enthusiasm. Everybody getting all excited about the Soviets launching a rocket ship! Everyone ought to be suspicious. It might just drop a bomb on us as it flies by.

GRANDPA: That's not possible. Any object discharged from Sputnik would burn up as it re-enters Earth's atmosphere.

MYRA: Stop teaching me science, Dad. I'm out of school, and so are you!

GRANDPA: Sorry, Myra. I didn't mean to—

MYRA: All this fuss over the Commies showing off. These are the same kind of people that killed Jeff in Korea. How am I supposed to celebrate their... their Sputnik?

GRANDPA: I fully understand, Myra. It must be hard for you.

MYRA: It's getting colder out here. I'm not staying out to see some Commie satellite. I've got better things to do. *(AGATHA ENTERS LEFT, wearing a yellow sweater and carrying a brown one. She is followed by SUSAN, who wears a skirt and blouse and carries a textbook.)*

AGATHA: Here you go, Grandpa. This'll keep you nice and warm.

GRANDPA: Thank you, dear.

SUSAN: Grandpa, can you help me with my Earth Science homework?

AGATHA: Isn't that cheating?

SUSAN: Shut up, Agatha.

GRANDPA: I'd be happy to, Susan. Right after Sputnik passes by. It ought to be along any time now.

SUSAN: *(Disappointed.)* All right... *(Starts to go back in the house.)*

GRANDPA: You should stay and see this, Susan. It's better than science homework. It's science history being made!

MYRA: *(Disgusted.)* History! Honestly, Dad.

AGATHA: I wish we had a telescope!

GRANDPA: We'll see it all the same.

MYRA: Susan, did you dry those dishes and put them away?

SUSAN: I'll do it later.

MYRA: *(Irritable.)* Susan Tolman, you march right into that kitchen and do it now!

SUSAN: All right... All right... *(EXITS LEFT.)*

MYRA: Dad, put that sweater on right now! I don't want you ending up in the hospital!

GRANDPA: Oh, I forgot. *(Puts on the sweater.)* Sorry, Myra.

MYRA: And zip it up! *(EXITS LEFT.)*

AGATHA: What's wrong with Mama tonight?

GRANDPA: I'm afraid this whole Soviet thing... Well, it brings back hurtful memories.

AGATHA: About Daddy?

GRANDPA: Yes. *(Pause.)* Almost time now.

AGATHA: Which way do I look?

GRANDPA: *(Points.)* To the southern sky.

AGATHA: It must be huge for us to see it way down here.

GRANDPA: Actually Sputnik is only fifty-eight centimeters in diameter.

AGATHA: How big is that?

GRANDPA: Oh... about the size of a beach ball.

AGATHA: Really?

GRANDPA: Its exterior is polished metal, so it reflects the light from the sun and emits quite a beam of light.

AGATHA: But the sun isn't out. It's dark!

GRANDPA: Well, Sputnik is orbiting 560 miles above Earth's surface. That's so high up that the satellite is still in the light of the sun. And it's moving fast. About eighteen thousand miles per hour.

AGATHA: That sounds awful fast. Won't it go by so fast we'll miss it?

GRANDPA: Not at that distance. We ought to be able to watch it for a whole minute or two before it orbits out of sight.

AGATHA: Grandpa, is this really science history?

GRANDPA: It sure is. Just like the Wright Brothers and Charles Lindbergh.

AGATHA: We learned about him in school. Lindbergh. He flew over the Atlantic Ocean.

GRANDPA: Solo. Yes, he was quite an aviator. I saw him once.

AGATHA: Fly over the ocean?

GRANDPA: *(Laughs.)* No. I was still teaching in Utah back in 1927. Your grandmother and I saw him in Chicago in 1939. He was giving a speech.

AGATHA: Did you ever see the Wright Brothers?

GRANDPA: *(Laughs.)* Afraid not. They didn't give speeches.

AGATHA: I've never seen anyone famous. How could I, living in Oklahoma City?

GRANDPA: Agatha, you're going to see something very famous tonight.

AGATHA: That's right! Sputnik!

GRANDPA: Someday you will be able to tell your children and your grandchildren— *(Looks up.)* Wait a minute! I think this is it!

AGATHA: *(Excited.)* Really? Where? Where?

GRANDPA: *(Points.)* You see that little light moving just over the horizon?

AGATHA: Where?

GRANDPA: *(Turns her head the right direction.)* Over there. It looks like the light on an airplane. But it's moving much faster. See it there?

AGATHA: I see it!

GRANDPA: Look at how fast it's moving! Like a shooting star!

AGATHA: I can actually see it!

GRANDPA: Isn't it beautiful?

AGATHA: It sure is! *(Rushes to the door, opens it, and yells OFF.)* Mama! Susan! It's here! You can see it! It's Sputnik! *(Rushes back to GRANDPA.)* It sure is moving fast!

SUSAN: *(ENTERS LEFT with a dish towel in her hand.)* Let me see. Where is it?

AGATHA: *(Points.)* Up there!

GRANDPA: *(Points.)* You see that light just above those telephone poles? The light that's moving?

SUSAN: No... Oh, yes, now I do! *(MYRA quietly opens the door and stands in the doorway looking at the sky.)* How do you know it's Sputnik? Maybe it's an airplane.

AGATHA: Moving so fast? Grandpa says it's going eighteen thousand miles an hour!

GRANDPA: Look how it's practically across the sky already!

AGATHA: "Faster than a speeding bullet!"

SUSAN: The way it's moving, it'll be gone in a minute.

GRANDPA: Just about so. But it will be back in less than two hours. *(Shakes his head in disbelief.)* Orbiting Earth… the first man-made object to ever orbit Earth.

AGATHA: *(Slow.)* Wow… *(ALL stare into the sky. MYRA stands in the doorway and weeps. LIGHTS SLOWLY FADE OUT.)*

AFTERMATH

Sputnik 1 orbited Earth for twenty-two days before its battery power ran out. The satellite continued circling the planet until it fell to Earth on January 4, 1958, burning up as it re-entered Earth's atmosphere after 1,440 completed revolutions. The success of the Russian Sputnik 1 prompted the United States to invest more money and people in its space program, and the Space Race between the two countries began. In 1961, the Soviet Union was the first nation to put a man in space. A month later, President Kennedy challenged America to send a man to the moon (and return him back safely) before the end of the decade. In July of 1969, the United States accomplished this goal and became the first nation to put a man on the surface of the moon.

ADIOS, HAVANA
(1959)

BACKGROUND

A revolutionary movement on the island nation of Cuba began in 1953 under the leadership of Fidel Castro. The revolt gradually gained power, and on January 1, 1959, the rebels ousted Cuban President Fulgencio Batista and took over the government. The result was the first Communist nation in the Western Hemisphere, a direct threat to the United States.

SETTING

TIME: An early evening in 1959.
PLACE: The living room of a middle-class family in Minneapolis, Minnesota.

CHARACTERS

MELVIN (M)................................. hotel manager and family man
MARGERY (F)............................. his wife
DEBBIE (F) .... their sixteen-year-old daughter
SKIPPER (M) .... their eleven-year-old son
LLOYD (M).................................. their eighteen-year-old son
MR. BIXBY (M) .... Melvin's boss

SET DESCRIPTION

The living room is set with furnishings of the period, including a television set. The front door to the outside is RIGHT, and an archway leading to the kitchen and other parts of the house is LEFT.

PROPERTIES

Magazine (DEBBIE); oily rag (LLOYD); dishcloth (MARGERY).

SOUND EFFECTS

Doorbell, canned laughter.

LIGHTS UP on SKIPPER, sitting on the floor watching TV. He wears dungarees and a plaid shirt. DEBBIE sits nearby, looking through a magazine. She wears a skirt and a fluffy sweater. MELVIN ENTERS LEFT from the kitchen. He wears a white shirt and tie with a comfortably worn sweater.

MELVIN: Skipper, turn off that television. *(Calls OFF LEFT.)* Margery, leave those dishes 'til later.

MARGERY: *(From OFF LEFT.)* In a minute, Melvin...

MELVIN: *(To DEBBIE.)* How come you aren't helping your mother with the dishes?

DEBBIE: 'Cause you said for everyone to come in the living room for a family powwow or something.

MELVIN: A family meeting. An important one. Where is Lloyd?

DEBBIE: Probably working on the car. Like always. *(SKIPPER laughs out loud at something on the TV.)*

MELVIN: Skipper, I said to turn off the television.

SKIPPER: Aw, Dad. It's Uncle Miltie!

MELVIN: I don't care if it's Uncle Sam. *(Turns off the TV.)* This is important. *(Calls out.)* Margery!

MARGERY: *(From OFF LEFT.)* Coming!

DEBBIE: The last time we had a family meeting, it was just to tell us you traded in the Chevy for a station wagon.

MELVIN: This is even more important. *(Calls OFF RIGHT.)* Lloyd!

LLOYD: *(ENTERS RIGHT, wiping his greasy hands on an oily rag. He wears dirty pants and a t-shirt.)* I'm here. This better be good. I'm in the middle of changing the oil.

MELVIN: Leave that jalopy of yours alone and sit down. *(Calls OFF LEFT.)* Margery!

MARGERY: *(ENTERS LEFT, wiping her wet hands with a dishcloth. She wears a housedress and an apron.)* I'm right here, Melvin. I just had to let that casserole pan soak 'til later. What's all the fuss?

SKIPPER: Yeah. What's going on?

LLOYD: Not a new station wagon, I hope. *(Sits.)*

DEBBIE: Station wagons are so uncool.

MELVIN: Sit down, Margery. Right here. *(Points to an armchair.)*

MARGERY: Are you sure, Melvin?

SKIPPER: But that's Dad's chair.

MELVIN: Sit!

MARGERY: *(Sits.)* Melvin, you're frightening me! What is this all about?

DEBBIE: Spill, Daddy-O!

MELVIN: I didn't want to say anything until it was official, but today it became official.

MARGERY: What did, dear?

MELVIN: *(Proud.)* Your husband... *(To the CHILDREN.)* Your father, children, has been named the new general manager of the Hilton Hotel in—

DEBBIE: Uh-oh...

LLOYD: Yes?

MELVIN: In Havana! The Havana Hilton! One of the prides of the chain. *(Awkward pause.)*

DEBBIE: There's a Hilton in Havana, Minnesota?

SKIPPER: Cuba, you dummy!

MARGERY: Skipper, don't call your sister a dummy.

MELVIN: Right on the beach. The jewel of Havana!

DEBBIE: We're going to move to Cuba?

MELVIN: We'll be living in the general manager's suite. Sixteen stories up and overlooking the pool.

MARGERY: Melvin, dear, I wish you had discussed this with me first.

LLOYD: Isn't there a revolution or something going on in Cuba?

MELVIN: A little political misunderstanding. Nothing to concern ourselves about.

SKIPPER: We can't move! I just got on the junior hockey team!

DEBBIE: And what about all my friends?

SKIPPER: And my friends!

DEBBIE: You don't have any friends, you twerp! I have dozens!

MARGERY: Don't call your brother a—

MELVIN: They can all visit you in Havana. Compliments of the house.

MARGERY: Melvin, this is all so sudden. I had no idea—

MELVIN: I told you I was in line for a promotion. It was down to three managers in the Hilton system. I didn't say anything, because I didn't want to jinx it.

SKIPPER: Do they even have hockey in Cuba?

LLOYD: Sure. They call it water polo.

MARGERY: What about school for the children?

DEBBIE: I can't go to a Cuban school. I got a C minus in Spanish last semester!

MELVIN: There's an English-speaking school for all the American families that are in Havana. It is rumored to be excellent.

SKIPPER: Do they have hockey?

MARGERY: I don't think so, dear.

LLOYD: I don't care how excellent. I want to graduate from Walter Johnson High!

MELVIN: You will, Lloyd. We don't move until June fifth.

MARGERY: That's less than five months away!

MELVIN: Enough time to sell the house and—

DEBBIE: Sell the house! You mean, we're not ever coming back?

MELVIN: Oh, maybe someday. We'll put in storage whatever we don't take with us.

SKIPPER: Can I bring my stuffed frog collection?

LLOYD: And what about my hot rod?

DEBBIE: If Lloyd can bring his jalopy, I want to bring Mary Jane!

LLOYD: You can't bring a pony to Cuba!

DEBBIE: Oh, yeah? *(The CHILDREN begin to argue loudly.)*

MAGERY: Enough, children! I said enough! *(They stop.)*

MELVIN: We have plenty of time to work out the details. The important thing right now is that we celebrate our good fortune! We're going to Havana! *(Awkward pause.)*

DEBBIE: I wish it was just a new station wagon.

MARGERY: Now, now, children. Let's look on the positive side.

MELVIN: We'll be on the beach! And in the finest hotel in all Havana!

DEBBIE: *(Sour.)* Yippee… *(SOUND EFFECT: DOORBELL.)*

MARGERY: Who can that be?

MELVIN: I can't imagine. *(Crosses RIGHT to the door.)*

SKIPPER: One of Debbie's dozens of friends.

DEBBIE: One of your stuffed frogs!

MELVIN: *(Opens the door.)* Mr. Bixby! Come on in!

BIXBY: *(ENTERS RIGHT, wearing a suit.)* Sorry to intrude at your home, Melvin, but I didn't want to tell you over the phone.

MELVIN: Tell me what? Margery, you remember Mr. Bixby? Vice-president in charge of overseas operations.

MARGERY: Welcome, Mr. Bixby. Come in.

MELVIN: Yes, come in and sit down!

BIXBY: I can only stay a minute. There will be a meeting about this tomorrow at ten, but I wanted you to know right away. Can we talk in private, Melvin?

MARGERY: If this concerns Melvin's job, I think the whole family should hear.

LLOYD: Yeah.

BIXBY: Well...

MELVIN: Go ahead, Mr. Bixby. I was just telling my family about Havana and—

BIXBY: That's what I'm here about.

MELVIN: Oh? *(Brief pause.)*

BIXBY: It all comes down to this, Melvin. It's gone.

MELVIN: What's gone?

BIXBY: The Havana Hilton. It's gone.

MARGERY: What?

SKIPPER: Someone stole a hotel?

LLOYD: They blew it up, didn't they? Those revolutionaries.

BIXBY: No. But they might as well have.

MELVIN: I don't understand.

BIXBY: This afternoon, Castro and the Communist Party confiscated all American property and businesses in Cuba. It's all gone. The GM plant. The Westinghouse offices. The Shell refineries. Even the American Embassy. Castro took it all.

MELVIN: But... but... they can't do that.

BIXBY: They did. The State Department has ordered all Americans out of Cuba immediately. The whole country has fallen to the Commies.

SKIPPER: Wow...

LLOYD: Communists in North America?

MARGERY: I can't believe it.

BIXBY: I'm just glad this all happened before you moved your family down there, Melvin.

MELVIN: *(Stunned.)* Yes...

BIXBY: We're having a hell of a time getting Schneider and his family out. They were kicked out of the hotel a few hours ago and are hiding with the Westinghouse families.

MARGERY: How horrible!

MELVIN: *(Still in shock.)* The finest hotel in Havana...

BIXBY: Was. The Commies will probably turn it into a commune or something.

MARGERY: *(Hugs MELVIN.)* Oh, my dear! I know how terribly disappointed you must feel.

BIXBY: Better off here in Minneapolis. You're doing a great job managing the Hilton here.

MELVIN: Thank you.

DEBBIE: So everything's okay then?

SKIPPER: I can play hockey!

MARGERY: Melvin, it's all for the best.

LLOYD: Not really, Mom. Do you know what this means? Castro taking over?

DEBBIE: I think I'll switch from Spanish to French!

BIXBY: Your boy is right, Melvin. This Castro thing is bad news. For all of us.

LLOYD: Communists right in our backyard.

BIXBY: Cuba is only ninety miles off the coast of Florida.

SKIPPER: I'm sure glad we live in Minnesota!

BIXBY: Now that Cuba has gone Communist, those Ruskies are going to get very friendly with Castro. Already are. Heck, the Soviets were probably behind the revolution.

LLOYD: The Russians can send troops to Cuba. They might even send missiles. Only ninety miles from our country. It's not good.

BIXBY: You said it, son. Well, I have to run. I got some other calls to make. The Stock Market has gone crazy since this afternoon. We've got to protect the Hilton stock. See you at the meeting at ten tomorrow morning, Melvin. Good night, all.

MELVIN: *(Opens the front door.)* Good night, Mr. Bixby.

MARGERY: Thank you for coming and telling us the news personally.

BIXBY: The least I could do. Good night. *(EXITS RIGHT. MELVIN closes the door. A long silence.)*

MARGERY: As I say, Melvin, it's all for the best.

LLOYD: Sure. The Commies take over another country. Just like North Korea... Indochina. Where's it going to end? Nuclear war?

MARGERY: Stop, Lloyd. You're frightening the children.

MELVIN: Enough.

LLOYD: Sorry, Mom. *(Another pause.)*

SKIPPER: I ain't scared of no Commies!

MARGERY: Don't say ain't, Skipper. You know better.

SKIPPER: Sorry, Mom. *(Another pause.)*

MELVIN: *(Weary.)* Well, what's done is done. Family meeting over. Go back to… whatever you were doing. Debbie, go help your mother with those dishes.

DEBBIE: Okay, Dad. *(Rises and heads OFF LEFT with MARGERY.)*

LLOYD: I gotta finish working on the car. *(EXITS RIGHT.)*

MELVIN: Skipper?

SKIPPER: Yes, Dad?

MELVIN: I think Milton Berle is still on. You can turn the television set back on.

SKIPPER: Thanks, Dad! *(Turns on the TV and sits on floor. SOUND EFFECT: CANNED LAUGHTER.)*

MELVIN: I think I'll join you… *(Sits. LIGHTS FADE OUT.)*

AFTERMATH

Relations between Communist Cuba and the United States were very tense after the revolution, particularly when American holdings in Cuba were confiscated by Castro. Matters were even more strained after the unsuccessful attempt by the CIA to invade Cuba in 1961 (known as the Bay of Pigs Invasion), and the Soviet Union's attempt to place nuclear missiles in Cuba in October of 1962 (known as the Cuban Missile Crisis).

ALL MY LOVING
(1964)

BACKGROUND

Having become famous in America with their records, the British rock group, the Beatles, arrived at Kennedy Airport in New York City on February 7, 1964, where they were greeted by three thousand screaming fans. The group was booked to appear two days later on *The Ed Sullivan Show*, where they would perform five songs on that Sunday's live broadcast. For many Americans, this was the first time they would actually see the Beatles perform.

SETTING

TIME: Sunday, February 9, 1964.

PLACE: The basement of Sheree, a high school girl, in the suburbs
of Rochester, New York.

CHARACTERS

SHEREE (F) .... high school girl
BETTY (F) .... another
PATTY (F) .... another
MARIE (F) .... another
SHEREE'S MOTHER (F) .... offstage voice
SHEREE'S FATHER (M) .... offstage voice

SET DESCRIPTION

The basement has been finished off as a rec room with a sofa, chairs, a dartboard, a refrigerator with bottles of soda, and a television set with rabbit ear antennas. A bottle opener is on a coffee table.

PROPERTIES

Beatles magazine, plate of brownies, working Polaroid camera on a strap (MARIE); Beatles magazine, plate of brownies, bottle of cream soda (BETTY); plate of Rice Krispie treats, watch (SHEREE).

LIGHTS UP on MARIE and BETTY, sitting on the sofa, each paging through a Beatles magazine. MARIE has a Polaroid camera on a strap around her neck. It is 7:50 in the evening.

MARIE: John is the cutest! No contest!

BETTY: Paul!

MARIE: John!

BETTY: How can you say John Lennon is cuter than Paul McCartney? Nobody in the world is cuter than Paul! Not even Pat Boone!

MARIE: John's face has character!

BETTY: Character? What does that have to do with anything?! *(Sticks her magazine in front of MARIE'S face.)* Look at that face! Paul is like the epoxy of cute!

MARIE: I think you mean epitome.

BETTY: *(Mocks.)* Sorry! But I don't have to be on the honor roll like you, Marie, to know who is cute!

MARIE: I'm not saying Paul McCartney is not cute—

BETTY: Don't even breathe such a thought!

MARIE: Betty, there is more to life than just being cute.

BETTY: *(Belligerent.)* Like what?!

MARIE: Forget it. Why did you bring your father's Polaroid? Party pictures?

BETTY: To take photos of the Beatles, stupid!

MARIE: *(Sarcastic.)* I didn't know they were coming over. I thought it was just Patty and Sheree and us. I would have shampooed my hair.

BETTY: On the television, you moron!

MARIE: You're going to take pictures of them on TV?

BETTY: Yeah!

MARIE: We've got dozens of pictures in these magazines! Besides, I don't think they would turn out very well.

BETTY: I want pictures of them on *The Ed Sullivan Show*!

MARIE: There will be hundreds of those on sale in magazines tomorrow! Color ones even!

BETTY: I want… personal pictures.

MARIE: Personal? Betty, you're not going to stick your head next to the screen and make us take your picture with the Beatles?

BETTY: Maybe.

MARIE: *(Disgusted.)* Honestly, Betty!

SHEREE: *(ENTERS RIGHT with a plate of Rice Krispie treats.)* The brownies won't be ready for a few more minutes. But look! Rice Krispies treats!

BETTY: Great! I'm starving! *(Helps herself.)*

SHEREE: *(Looks at her watch.)* Eight more minutes, girls!

MARIE: Isn't Patty coming?

SHEREE: Any second. I know she doesn't want to miss this!

BETTY: *(Mouth full.)* I read that they are going to be on at the very beginning of the show!

MARIE: I hope they sing "All My Loving." That's my favorite.

BETTY: Do you honestly believe that "All My Loving" is a better song than "She Loves You"?

MARIE: Yes!

BETTY: Why? *(Mocks.)* 'Cause it has more "character"?

MARIE: Maybe, yes!

SHEREE: Are you two at it again? Who's thirsty? *(Crosses to the refrigerator.)* We've got Coke and RC Cola and some kind of root beer and—

BETTY: No cream soda?

SHEREE: I don't know. I'll check.

MARIE: Coke is fine for me.

BETTY: Sheree, can you believe Marie thinks John Lennon is cuter than Paul McCartney?

SHEREE: *(Head in the refrigerator.)* No cream soda. But we've got Orange Crush.

BETTY: Yuck! Give me an RC.

SHEREE: *(Closes the refrigerator and brings them their bottles of soda.)* I'm kinda undecided. Paul is cute, no question. But I like the tall, dark, and handsome type.

BETTY: Ringo?

SHEREE: George Harrison, you goof! *(Hands the bottle opener to MARIE.)* Here's the opener.

MARIE: Thanks.

PATTY: *(ENTERS RIGHT. Her enthusiasm seems a bit forced.)* I didn't miss anything, did I?

BETTY: Just Marie going on about John Lennon's "character."

SHEREE: Still six more minutes, Patty. What took you so long?

PATTY: Long story. Forget it.

BETTY: *(To PATTY.)* You want a Rice Krispies treat? They're fresh! Sheree's mom made them.

PATTY: Uh…

MARIE: Patty, what's the better song? "All My Loving" or "She Loves You"?

PATTY: *(Distracted.)* What? Oh… I hadn't thought about it.

BETTY: Who's your favorite Beatle, then? You must have thought about that!

PATTY: Uh… Paul's awfully cute.

BETTY: *(Triumphant.)* I rest my case!

SHEREE: What do you want to drink, Patty?

PATTY: Oh… nothing right now.

BETTY: Just warning you. There's no cream soda.

MOTHER: *(From OFF RIGHT.)* Girls, the fudge brownies are ready! I need someone to cut them. Come on up!

SHEREE: Okay, Mom!

BETTY: Fudge brownies! Great!

SHEREE: Will you go get them, Betty?

BETTY: Sure! *(Gets up from the sofa.)*

SHEREE: And Marie, you better go too.

BETTY: I know how to cut brownies!

SHEREE: My mom always goes overboard, so I'm sure there will be more than one plate.

MARIE: Two plates of brownies?! I'm going!

BETTY: *(To MARIE.)* I know when we're getting the bum's rush. They want to talk about us behind our backs.

SHEREE: And ask my mom if there's any cream soda up there.

BETTY: Righto! *(EXITS RIGHT with MARIE.)*

PATTY: What was that all about?

SHEREE: What's going on, Patty? You look terrible.

PATTY: Thanks.

SHEREE: You been crying or something? Your eyes are all red.

PATTY: Is it that obvious? *(Sits on the sofa.)* I shouldn't have come.

SHEREE: What's happened? *(Sits next to her.)*

PATTY: Everything. Everything awful, that is. *(Sincere.)* My whole life is gonna change.

SHEREE: Patty!

PATTY: Mom and Dad told me tonight that they are getting a divorce.

SHEREE: A divorce! Your parents? But they're the most... most... married people I know.

PATTY: Weird, isn't it? They never fight. They hardly ever argue about anything. Except maybe money. They said they haven't been in love with each other for a long time, and they're tired of pretending.

SHEREE: Well, they sure put on a convincing front. All the times I stayed over at your house, I never once suspected... a divorce!

PATTY: That's not the worst of it.

SHEREE: What?

PATTY: Mom not only wants custody of me and Jerry, but she wants to move back to Arizona where her family is.

SHEREE: Arizona! That's like... a million miles away from Rochester! They can't do that!

PATTY: Dad is moving out of the house right away. Mom will let me finish my senior year here, then this summer, we move.

SHEREE: But you're my best friend!

PATTY: Don't start me crying again! I didn't want to come tonight, but I knew everyone would suspect something if I didn't. And I had to tell you, Sheree.

SHEREE: *(Tears up.)* Now it's my turn to cry!

PATTY: Promise me you won't? I don't want Marie and Betty to know. Not yet.

SHEREE: I don't know what to say. I'm in some kind of shock!

PATTY: So am I, but let's not show it in front of the others.

SHEREE: Those two are so crazy tonight over the Beatles being on *Ed Sullivan* that they won't notice us at all. Betty actually brought a camera to take pictures!

PATTY: Of us all?

SHEREE: *(Laughs.)* No! Of the Beatles on TV!

BETTY: *(ENTERS RIGHT with MARIE, each carrying a plate of brownies. BETTY also carries a bottle of cream soda.)* Don't drop those brownies, Marie!

MARIE: You just be careful with your plate, Miss Klutz!

SHEREE: Just about time, girls! I'll let the TV warm up. *(Turns on the television.)*

BETTY: Look! *(Holds up a bottle.)* Cream soda! *(Nearly drops the plate of brownies.)*

MARIE: I said be careful, Betty!

SHEREE: Can I get you something to drink now, Patty?

PATTY: Sure. *(SHEREE goes to the refrigerator.)*

BETTY: I got the last cream soda. Sorry, Patty.

SHEREE: How about Orange Crush?

PATTY: Fine.

BETTY: Yuck!

SHEREE: *(Closes the refrigerator and gives a bottle to PATTY.)* Where's the opener?

BETTY: I've got it here. *(Hands the opener to PATTY.)* Here, Patty.

PATTY: Thanks.

MARIE: See if you can adjust the rabbit ears, Sheree. The screen's a bit fuzzy. *(SHEREE goes to the television and moves the antennas a bit.)*

BETTY: I don't want my pictures to be fuzzy!

SHEREE: Better?

MARIE: Yeah. *(To PATTY.)* Can you believe Betty brought her father's Polaroid?

BETTY: I want to remember the moment. Anything wrong with that? Smile, Marie! *(Takes a photos with the Polaroid, and then a photo rolls out.)*

MARIE: Betty! I had my mouth full of brownie!

SHEREE: Oh, I want to see that!

BETTY: First we have to wait thirty-five seconds for it to develop.

PATTY: Shake it a little and it will develop faster.

BETTY: Really? *(Shakes the photo.)*

SHEREE: Next we'll do a picture of Betty with Rice Krispies up her nose!

BETTY: Gross!

MARIE: Sheree, your mom sure knows how to make good fudge brownies.

SHEREE: It's just a brownie box mix, but she makes the fudge herself. Have one, Patty.

PATTY: Sure.

BETTY: Ed Sullivan is such a square. How did he get the Beatles to come on his show?

MARIE: Maybe he's a Beatles fan?

SHEREE: Oh, sure. Like my father is a Beatles fan!

BETTY: He is?

MARIE: Betty, don't you know what sarcasm is?

BETTY: Stuff it, Miss Honor Roll. *(Looks at the photo.)* Hey, the picture is forming!

MARIE: Let me see it! *(Gathers around BETTY with SHEREE, looks at the photo, and laughs.)* I look awful!

SHEREE: That goes in the yearbook! *(Takes the photo to PATTY.)* Look at this, Patty! *(Both laugh.)*

BETTY: Hey, you two! *(To SHEREE and PATTY.)* Don't move! *(Takes their picture together, and the photo rolls out.)*

SHEREE: Betty!

MARIE: At least the two of you didn't have a mouth stuffed with brownies!

BETTY: I'll put this one in my scrapbook and label it "best friends"! Now all we do is wait thirty-five seconds—

MARIE: *(Looking at the TV.)* Look! It's starting!

SHEREE: It is!

BETTY: *(Shouts.)* Paul, I love you!

MARIE: He can't hear you, Betty.

FATHER: *(From OFF RIGHT.)* Cut out that racket down there!

MARIE: *(Quiet.)* I still prefer John! *(BLACKOUT.)*

AFTERMATH

The appearance of the Beatles on *The Ed Sullivan Show* drew 73 million viewers, a record for a TV broadcast at the time. The Beatles also appeared the following two Sundays on the program (one live and the other taped), toured the States, and then returned to England as the most popular rock group in the world. Their appearance was a pop culture phenomenon that launched the "British Invasion" in the United States. In 1970, the group broke up, ending the most popular collaboration in the history of modern music. On the night of December 8, 1980, John Lennon was assassinated outside his Manhattan apartment in New York.

A TRIANGLE BOX FRAME
(1972)

BACKGROUND

The United States started sending American troops, labeled "military advisors," to French Indochina in 1950 to fight in the war between the Communist government in the North and the democratic government in the South. By 1962, when the country was known as Vietnam and divided into North and South, there were thousands of American troops in Vietnam helping South Vietnam fight the Communist Viet Cong in the North. In 1968, over 16,000 American soldiers died fighting in Vietnam, escalating the massive anti-war movement in the United States. That year, Richard Nixon was elected president with the promise of ending the Vietnam War, but the number of American troops in Vietnam did not begin to de-escalate until 1972, and the conflict continued for another year.

SETTING

TIME: August 1972.

PLACE: The living room of a middle-class family in suburban St. Louis, Missouri.

CHARACTERS

MELVIN (M)................................. aging hotel manager

LLOYD (M)................................... his adult son

DONNA (F)................................... Lloyd's wife

DEBBIE (F) .... Melvin's adult daughter

MARGERY (F)............................... Melvin's wife

SET DESCRIPTION

The living room is set with furnishings of the period. The front door is RIGHT, and an archway leading to the kitchen and other parts of the house is LEFT.

PROPERTIES

Purse containing a bottle of pills, American flag folded into a regulation triangle shape (MARGERY); glass of water (MELVIN); purse (DEBBIE).

LIGHTS UP on the living room of the middle-class suburban home of MELVIN and MARGERY. (We first met this family in the *Adios, Havana* scene [1959]. Melvin now manages a Hilton in St. Louis.) The FAMILY quietly ENTERS RIGHT through the front door. MELVIN wears a dark blue suit, white shirt, and tie. LLOYD years a dark green shirt, a dark blue blazer, and jeans. His pregnant wife DONNA wears a gray maternity dress and comfortable shoes. DEBBIE wears a black skirt and a short-sleeve dark blue blouse. MARGERY wears a simple black dress and heels. She carries her purse and an American flag folded into a regulation triangle shape. No one speaks as they enter. MELVIN sits and loosens his tie as LLOYD helps DONNA to the sofa, where she sits. He then takes off his blazer and tosses it on the back of a chair. MARGERY puts her purse down, but remains standing as she clutches the flag.

MELVIN: I thought that rain early this morning might cool things off. It just made it more humid. But it's a good thing the rain stopped before the service began.

LLOYD: At least that funeral director ordered enough chairs for the family. I don't think Donna could have stood so long.

DONNA: Stop fussing over me, Lloyd. I'm fine.

DEBBIE: If no one minds, I'm going to change into something cooler. *(Silence.)* All right, then. *(EXITS LEFT.)*

MELVIN: Margery, did you notice? Just about the whole hockey team was there.

DONNA: What hockey team?

LLOYD: His high school team. I recognized a lot of them.

MELVIN: *(To MARGERY.)* Wasn't that nice of them? To show up after—what is it now?—six years after graduating.

LLOYD: Five, I think. *(To DONNA.)* Skipper was a hell of a hockey player in high school.

MELVIN: Made captain of the team.

LLOYD: That was in Minneapolis, Dad. Right before we moved.

MELVIN: Well, he should have been captain here in St. Louis, too. He was the best player on the team. Was named most valuable player. We've got his trophy somewhere around here.

DONNA: *(To MARGERY.)* Mom, why don't you sit? You look exhausted.

LLOYD: What else can you expect in this heat? *(Goes to MARGERY.)* Come and sit over here, Mom. *(Brings her to an armchair, and she sits.)*

MELVIN: That minister said some nice things. But he went on too long.

LLOYD: *(Bitter.)* Nothing but a bunch of patriotic clichés. I'll bet he's got the same spiel for every—for all these kind of funerals. My guess is the Army writes the speeches and mails them out by the thousands.

MELVIN: Don't start, Lloyd. Think of your mother.

LLOYD: *(Testy.)* I'm thinking of Skipper! And Mom. And you and... and the whole damn country.

DEBBIE: *(ENTERS LEFT, wearing shorts and a tank top.)* This feels better. I thought I was gonna pass out while that preacher kept babbling on.

MELVIN: *(Gets angry.)* He was "babbling on" about your dead brother!

LLOYD: He didn't even know Skipper. He was just mouthing off about "God and country."

DEBBIE: Is Lloyd on his soapbox again?

LLOYD: Yes, if you want to know!

DEBBIE: I've heard it all before. I'm going to my room. Pete is supposed to call.

DONNA: Who's Pete? I thought you were dating Mark.

DEBBIE: I was, but I'm not. Now it's Pete. *(EXITS LEFT.)*

MELVIN: Your sister doesn't sound very upset.

DONNA: She is. She just doesn't want to show it.

LLOYD: She and Skipper were so close. I remember she cried when he enlisted. Believe me, she's upset about all this.

MELVIN: *(To LLOYD.)* And you? Are you upset? Or are you just angry?

LLOYD: I'm angry, all right. And you should be, too. And Mom— *(Stops himself. ALL look at MARGERY. An awkward pause.)*

MELVIN: *(Goes to MARGERY.)* Margery, would you like to go into the bedroom and lie down a bit? Get some rest? You haven't slept well ever since... well, for quite a long time. *(Pause.)*

MARGERY: *(Quiet.)* Timmy Garrity.

MELVIN: What's that, dear?

MARGERY: Timothy Garrity. He wasn't there today.

DONNA: Who's Timothy Garrity?

LLOYD: A kid on the hockey team. Back in high school.

MELVIN: I don't recall him. *(To MARGERY.)* You say he wasn't at the funeral? Well, there's a million and one reasons why he couldn't make it—

MARGERY: There's only one reason. He was killed in Vietnam three years ago.

MELVIN: Oh…

LLOYD: I remember Timmy Garrity. His older sister Sheila was in my class.

MARGERY: So Timmy couldn't be there today.

MELVIN: Margery, don't you think you ought to lie down? *(MARGERY stands, puts down the flag, goes over to her purse, and looks through it slowly.)*

DONNA: What are you looking for, Mom?

MARGERY: Pills. The ones the doctor gave me. They're in here somewhere.

DONNA: Bring it here. I'll find them for you. *(MARGERY brings the purse to DONNA, who looks through it.)*

MELVIN: That's a good idea, Margery. Something to calm you.

LLOYD: She seems pretty calm to me.

DONNA: *(Pulls out a pill bottle.)* These? Valium?

MARGERY: Yes. *(Takes the bottle.)*

MELVIN: Let me get you a glass of water, dear. *(EXITS RIGHT.)*

LLOYD: You've got to be careful with those, Mom. I hear they're addictive.

DONNA: They're just Valium, Lloyd.

MARGERY: I don't think they help much. But I don't think anything could help.

MELVIN: *(ENTERS RIGHT with a glass of water.)* Here you are, Margery. *(Hands her the glass.)*

MARGERY: Thank you, Melvin. *(Takes a pill and drinks some water.)*

DONNA: I know lots of people on Valium, Lloyd. It's safe enough.

MARGERY: Safe enough… what a nice idea. *(Hands the glass back to MELVIN.)* Thank you, dear. *(Sits again.)*

MELVIN: Now, I still think a little lie down in bed—

MARGERY: I just get headaches lying down. And if I sleep, I have nightmares.

MELVIN: Maybe with those pills—

MARGERY: I was thinking...

LLOYD: Yes, Mom?

MARGERY: How different it was when my eldest brother Hubert died in Okinawa. It was so different.

LLOYD: That's because he volunteered to go and knew what he was fighting for. Everyone knew during World War II. Not like this war. Nobody has a good reason for it.

MELVIN: *(Irritable.)* I think fighting for your country is reason enough!

LLOYD: *(Heated.)* Fighting for politicians, you mean. And dying because they won't admit that they're wrong. First LBJ, and now Nixon. All because they and most of the other jerks in Washington are too stubborn!

DONNA: *(Gentle.)* Lloyd! I don't think this is the right time—

LLOYD: When is the right time? After more funerals?

DONNA: I think you're upsetting your mother.

MELVIN: Yes!

MARGERY: Don't worry about me. It's all just words. All I know is my baby son is gone, and I still can't figure out why.

LLOYD: That's my whole point!

MELVIN: You're very brave, Margery. You're taking this tragedy like a good American.

LLOYD: *(Disgusted.)* A good American!

DONNA: Lloyd, I think we should go home. Lloyd Junior is not used to being with a babysitter all morning.

MARGERY: *(Tender.)* Poor little Lloyd. I'll bet he misses his mommy.

LLOYD: A little too much. But maybe we ought to go.

MELVIN: It might be for the best.

DONNA: *(Rises awkwardly.)* Please call if you need anything from us.

MELVIN: We're fine.

MARGERY: Where's Debbie? She ought to say goodbye.

LLOYD: *(Yells OFF LEFT.)* Debbie! We're leaving!

DEBBIE: *(From OFF LEFT.)* What? I'm on the phone!

MELVIN: *(Shouts OFF LEFT.)* Donna and Lloyd are leaving!

DEBBIE: *(From OFF LEFT.)* Bye! Give little Lloyd a big hug and kiss from me!

MELVIN: *(To MARGERY.)* No manners, that girl.

MARGERY: Give little Lloyd a kiss from me as well, Donna. And take care of yourself. You're in the most difficult trimester.

DONNA: *(Lighthearted.)* They're all difficult!

MELVIN: Goodbye, son.

LLOYD: *(To MARGERY.)* Take care of yourself, Mom.

MARGERY: I will, Lloyd. Goodbye.

DONNA: See you on Sunday, if not before.

MELVIN: Bye. *(LLOYD and DONNA EXIT RIGHT. MELVIN and MARGERY sit. Pause.)* Don't pay any attention to that nonsense Lloyd keeps spouting.

MARGERY: Nonsense? *(DEBBIE ENTERS LEFT with her purse.)*

MELVIN: Where are you going?

DEBBIE: Pete. *(To MARGERY.)* I hope you don't mind, Mom. I need to get out and talk to somebody about… all this.

MELVIN: You can stay here and talk to us.

DEBBIE: You know what I mean. Pete is easy to talk to. He's a very understanding guy.

MELVIN: That's what you said about Mark.

MARGERY: *(To DEBBIE.)* You go, dear. I understand.

DEBBIE: Thanks, Mom! *(Kisses her on the cheek.)* I won't be too late!

MARGERY: You're twenty-eight years old, Debbie. You don't have to answer to us.

MELVIN: She does as long as she lives under my roof!

DEBBIE: *(Kisses MELVIN on the cheek.)* Bye, Dad. *(EXITS RIGHT. Another awkward silence.)*

MARGERY: Melvin…

MELVIN: Yes, Margery?

MARGERY: *(Emotionless.)* I don't think I'm like you said. A good American.

MELVIN: Margery!

MARGERY: At least I don't feel like a good American. *(Picks up the folded flag.)* They took my baby boy, and all I have left is this flag.

MELVIN: Naturally you are devastated. So am I. But that doesn't mean—

MARGERY: *(Calm.)* My boy is gone. If Lloyd didn't have that heart murmur, they also would have taken him, and maybe he'd be gone now, too. I know I should be proud or something, but I'm not. I'm angry and bitter and very... very... fed up.

MELVIN: But you seem so calm. I don't understand.

MARGERY: *(Holds up the flag.)* What am I supposed to do with this?

MELVIN: They sell these triangle box frames. You put the folded flag in the box, and there's room for a photo, too. Maybe one with Skipper in his uniform. I see them in the stores all the time.

MARGERY: Smart business idea. Somebody's making money from all the grieving families. *(Shakes her head, then stands up and hands him the flag.)* Put it away someplace safe. But out of sight. I don't want to see it. I'd rather look at Skipper's hockey trophy. Where is it?

MELVIN: In the basement, I suppose.

MARGERY: Maybe tomorrow you can find it for me. *(Starts to weep.)* Oh, Melvin, what are we going to do? I don't think I can go on.

MELVIN: *(Rises and goes to her.)* I'll tell you what we're going to do. I'll go back to work at the Hilton, Lloyd will go back to work at the auto supply store, Donna will have her baby, and Debbie will finally stop dating every guy in sight and marry one of them. That's what we're going to do.

MARGERY: And me? What about me?

MELVIN: You can always go back to working at the library part time. Or volunteer again at the art museum. You can't give up living.

MARGERY: Oh, Melvin! *(Embraces him.)* Help me!

MELVIN: With anything you want.

MARGIE: Help me... to go on! *(They embrace desperately as the LIGHTS FADE OUT.)*

AFTERMATH

In August of 1973, the last American troops left Vietnam, and two years later, the North Vietnamese captured Saigon and the war ended, making the whole nation Communist. It is estimated that over 58,000 American soldiers died during the Vietnam War. It was the first war in American history in which the United States was not victorious. When the servicemen returned home, they were not treated like heroes. Ironically, it was never an officially declared war, but a "conflict" during the so-called Cold War in which Communist nations took the opposing side to the democratic nations.

Just Like a Toaster
(1973)

BACKGROUND

The history of computers goes back to calculating machines first developed in the nineteenth century. The modern computer, as we know it today, took shape during World War II, when code-deciphering machines began to retain numbers and started to compute combinations on their own. IBM introduced an early form of a computer at the 1939 New York World's Fair, and by the 1950s, computers were used to do accounting, inventory, and other functions for large businesses. The computers became smaller and more efficient in the 1960s, but the first "personal computer" that an individual could buy didn't become available until 1974. In the 1960s and early 1970s, the punch card system was still the most popular form of inputting information into computers. The operator used a keyboard to type out information, such as names and numbers, and the data translated into punch holes in thousands of cards that were fed into the computer. This was considered the most efficient and ingenious system at the time and was used by many companies around the world.

SETTING

TIME: April 1973.
PLACE: The basement computing center for a corporation in Buffalo, New York.

CHARACTERS

PEGGY FLYNN (F)...................... aging computer keypunch operator
PATTY (F)..................................... young keypunch operator

MRS. STEWART (F) .... supervisor of the computing
center

MICHAEL GAVIN (M) .... young IBM technician

SET DESCRIPTION

The room has two large punch card machines, each on its own DOWNSTAGE table. There's a chair at each table. Overhead lights make the room bright, but the basement has no windows. The door to the main hallway is LEFT.

SOUND EFFECTS

Typing, machine whirring.

FLEXIBLE CASTING NOTE

MRS. STEWART could be played by either gender with only minor script adjustments.

SOUND EFFECT: LOUD TYPING and MACHINE WHIRRING. LIGHTS UP on PATTY and PEGGY, their faces obscured as they each sit behind a bulky punch card machine. The equipment is rather noisy, so the ladies do not converse much while working. PATTY wears casual pants and a colorful blouse. PEGGY is dressed more conservatively in a skirt, blouse, and jacket. After a few moments, PATTY stops typing, stands, and turns her machine off. SOUND EFFECT: TYPING and MACHINE WHIRRING cuts in half.

PATTY: Five o'clock. I just barely got through "J." How are you doing?

PEGGY: *(Still typing behind the machine.)* Still on the letter "S."

PATTY: "S" is endless! Might as well quit now. I can't wait to get out of this cave and get some fresh air. I hate doing payroll.

PEGGY: *(Still types.)* I know the feeling.

PATTY: Walk you to the bus stop, Peggy?

PEGGY: *(Still types.)* Not tonight, Patty. I promised Mrs. Stewart I'd stick around for a while.

PATTY: Why?

PEGGY: I'm not exactly sure. *(Stops typing, stands, and turns off her machine. SOUND OUT.)* Some technician from IBM is coming to talk to the head office about the new system we're supposed to get.

PATTY: They need you for that?

PEGGY: Mrs. Stewart wants me to show this man how our current punch card system works. She said it won't take long.

PATTY: I hope you're getting overtime.

PEGGY: I'm not sure, but I'm glad Mrs. Stewart asked me to stay. I want to learn more about computers than just punching in cards. She knows it, and I think that's why she asked me to stay.

PATTY: Why is he coming after closing time?

PEGGY: Mrs. Stewart says that he's flying in from Pittsburgh. This is the soonest he can arrive.

PATTY: Well, good luck with it. They never tell us anything around here. Like what is this new system they are all excited about? I haven't a clue.

PEGGY: That's why I agreed to stay. Maybe I'll learn something. *(MRS. STEWART ENTERS LEFT. She wears a severe suit and looks much older than her years.)*

PATTY: Good night, Peggy. *(Passes by MRS. STEWART.)* Good night, Mrs. Stewart.

MRS. STEWART: Good night, Patty. *(PATTY EXITS LEFT.)* I wanted to remind you, Peggy, about staying a little late tonight.

PEGGY: I remembered. Any sign of this IBM man yet?

MRS. STEWART: I'm heading back up to the lobby to wait for him. I just wanted to check on you first.

PEGGY: I'll be here. I'm not sure what you want me to do, though.

MRS. STEWART: Show him how our current system works. A kind of demonstration.

PEGGY: No problem.

MRS. STEWART: Peggy, I know you want to move up from keypunch operator. This might be your opportunity.

PEGGY: *(Delighted.)* Thank you, Mrs. Stewart!

MRS. STEWART: I'll be back soon. *(Starts to EXIT.)* I hope he didn't get caught in traffic coming from the airport. *(EXITS LEFT.)*

PEGGY: *(To herself.)* Thank you indeed, Mrs. Stewart. Fifty-one years old, and I'm doing a job a high schooler could do. "I know you want to move up from keypunch operator." I sure do, Mrs. Stewart. I'm more than ready to move up. *(Paces.)* For the past ten years, I've only been moving sideways. If I could only get a crack at actually learning about computers, then... then... then maybe I'll stop talking to myself out loud!

MRS. STEWART: *(ENTERS LEFT with MICHAEL GAVIN. He is young but has a professional air about him. He is dressed in a fine suit that speaks of success.)* Right in here, Mr. Gavin. I want you to meet one of our keypunch operators, Peggy Flynn. *(PEGGY and MICHAEL immediately recognize each other and are shocked and embarrassed.)*

MICHAEL: *(Instinctive.)* Mom! *(Stops himself, then fumbles a bit as he tries to cover and regain his poise.)* My... my! *(Goes over to the machine.)* My, look at this. The IBM 029 Kanji Keypunch! I didn't know they were still being used.

MRS. STEWART: *(Having not noticed MICHAEL'S initial reaction.)* Peggy, this is Mr. Gavin from IBM in Pittsburgh.

PEGGY: *(Weak.)* Glad to meet you...

MICHAEL: *(Still looking at the machine and avoiding eye contact with PEGGY.)* Yes... the good old IBM 029.

MRS. STEWART: You must be very familiar with it?

MICHAEL: Actually, not. A bit before my time.

MRS. STEWART: Well, Peggy will demonstrate for you how the keypunch system works. *(PEGGY'S frozen.)* Isn't that right, Peggy?

PEGGY: *(Snaps out of it.)* Oh. Of course.

MRS. STEWART: Good. *(To MICHAEL.)* I have to make a few phone calls, then I'll be back to show you the mainframe and all.

MICHAEL: *(Still nervous.)* Ah... sure! The mainframe. That'll be great, thank you.

MRS. STEWART: If you'll excuse me for a moment, Peggy can answer any questions you might have. *(EXITS LEFT. Awkward pause.)*

PEGGY: *(Cautious.)* Hello, Michael.

MICHAEL: Mom.

PEGGY: This is a surprise.

MICHAEL: To say the least.

PEGGY: You look...

MICHAEL: Ten years older?

PEGGY: You look wonderful! A big shot technician for IBM! I'm very proud of you.

MICHAEL: Not such a big shot. At least not yet.

PEGGY: You look like a big success to me.

MICHAEL: Have you been living here in Buffalo since... since...?

PEGGY: Yes. I couldn't stay in Pittsburgh.

MICHAEL: I guess not.

PEGGY: How's Margy?

MICHAEL: She's fine. She liked going to college in Chicago so she stayed there. She's a social worker.

PEGGY: Wonderful! And your father?

MICHAEL: He died last year.

PEGGY: Oh.

MICHAEL: Some kind of stroke. And drugs. *(Awkward pause.)*

PEGGY: That doesn't surprise me.

MICHAEL: Mrs. Stewart says you can answer any questions I had.

PEGGY: *(Tentative.)* That's right.

MICHAEL: Well, here's a question for you—why did you walk out on us ten years ago?

PEGGY: I... I...

MICHAEL: Dad said it was another man.

PEGGY: *(Bitter laugh.)* He said that? There was no other man. He was the only man. And I was scared of him.

MICHAEL: Scared?

PEGGY: He tried to kill me. He was all doped up one night and tried to stab me with his hunting knife. I ran and never went back.

MICHAEL: And us? Margie and me? You left us with him?!

PEGGY: I knew he wouldn't hurt either of you. It was me he hated. Besides, you were already twenty and about to move out. And Margie was going off to college and... *(Shrugs.)* so I ran.

MICHAEL: But all these years! You never called or wrote or—!

PEGGY: I knew if I tried to contact you, he would find me. I didn't dare do anything but... disappear.

MICHAEL: So here you are. In Buffalo. Using your maiden name.

PEGGY: Yes. I've had all sorts of jobs here in town. None of them very good. But I am very interested in computers. I thought if I could get a job—any job—in a computer center, then maybe something would happen. Maybe. So far I've only got as far as keypunch operator.

MICHAEL: You better start looking for a different job. Keypunching is going out. Everything in computers is changing.

PEGGY: And there's no room for a fifty-one-year-old runaway mother. I know, this is a young person's business.

MICHAEL: It's not a matter of age. Everybody is going to be using computers soon.

PEGGY: *(In disbelief.)* What?

MICHAEL: They're not on the market yet, but they are developing small computers that will eventually be in every home! Just like a toaster or a TV set! And every business and school and organization with have them! They'll be everywhere! Computers will do everything from bookkeeping to controlling the air conditioning!

PEGGY: Michael, you astonish me!

MICHAEL: You don't believe me?

PEGGY: Oh, I believe every word you say. I am astonished at what you have made of yourself! And I like it very much.

MICHAEL: Mom...

PEGGY: I'm sorry for leaving you like that. I hope you don't hate me for it.

MRS. STEWART: *(ENTERS LEFT, briskly.)* And how are we getting along?

MICHAEL: Fine. Just fine.

MRS. STEWART: Did Peggy explain everything to you?

MICHAEL: Yes... very well.

MRS. STEWART: Thank you, Peggy. You can go home now—

MICHAEL: Actually, I would like... Mrs. Flynn to stay and hear what I have to tell you about the new system. She seems to have a very good grasp on computers, and I believe she might be very useful to you with the new system.

MRS. STEWART: My, that's quite a recommendation! Isn't it, Peggy?

PEGGY: It certainly is. Thank you... Mr. Gavin.

MICHAEL: Now the first thing to go are these old Kanji keypunch machines. The new system is called IBM 7090, and it doesn't use punch cards. The information is on a disk instead. It's an eight-inch vinyl disk. Looks like a small record but it's flexible. That's why they call them "floppy disks."

MRS. STEWART: Floppy disks! My, what a name!

MICHAEL: Each one of these disks can hold more information than six thousand punch cards!

MRS. STEWART: Amazing!

MICHAEL: And here's the beautiful part—a floppy disk is portable and can be used to input the same information to another computer. You can be working on a project at work, remove the disk, bring it home, and then continue to work on it on your home computer.

MRS. STEWART: *(Confused.)* Home computer?

PEGGY: Yes. I heard from a reliable source that sooner than we think we will all have small computers in our homes.

MRS. STEWART: I hadn't heard that. My, Peggy, you really are on top of things!

MICHAEL: With the new IMB 7090 system, a company can keep hundreds of floppy disks on file, thereby making the amount of information practically infinite! *(BLACKOUT.)*

AFTERMATH

The use of the floppy disk gradually made punch cards obsolete. When the first PCs ("personal computers") went on sale in 1974, information, games, and other programs were all on disks. CD-ROMs came soon after, and other developments followed. Thanks to the evolution of microchips, computers have continued to get smaller as their memory capacities have greatly increased. What used to be contained in a seven-ton computer in the 1950s doesn't even begin to fill the capacity of today's handheld tablets and phones.

APPENDIX OF PLAYS BY TOPIC

PLAY \ TOPIC	Economics	Cultural Arts	Black History	Immigration	War Time	Women's Rights	Aviation and Space	Health	Inventions
Without Ice									★
Her First Decision			★						
Laura Keene's Big Night		★			★				
The Good Fight						★			
Breaker Boy	★						★		
Beaded Souvenirs for Sale	★	★							
Music in the Air		★							★
The Letter E				★					
Caught in the Wire					★		★		
Tiny Pieces of Light									★
Lamp Chops and Pineapple		★							★
Bread and Soup	★								
Lady Lindy						★	★		
We Interrupt This Program		★							
Poison					★	★	★		
Sunday Morning					★				
Add One Cup of Sugar	★				★				
VJ Day Blues	★		★		★	★			
'Til Further Notice							★		
Waiting for the Bus			★						
About the Size of a Beach Ball							★		★
Adios, Havana					★				
All My Loving		★							
A Triangle Box Frame					★				
Just Like a Toaster									★

ABOUT THE AUTHOR

Thomas Hischak has written forty-three published plays, which are performed hundreds of times each year throughout the English-speaking world. His playwriting has been recognized with top honors from the Stanley Drama Awards (New York City) for *Cold War Comedy*, the Julie Harris Playwriting Award (Beverly Hills, California) for *The Cardiff Giant*, and the Association of American Community Theatres (AACT) NewPlayFest for *The Emperor of North America*. Hischak is also the author of twenty-seven non-fiction books about theatre, film, and popular music, including *The Oxford Companion to the American Musical, The Rodgers and Hammerstein Encyclopedia, The Tin Pan Alley Encyclopedia, Off-Broadway Musicals Since 1919, The Disney Song Encyclopedia, Word Crazy: Broadway Lyricists, American Literature on Stage and Screen, Theatre as Human Action, 100 Greatest American Plays,* and *The Oxford Companion to American Theatre.* Besides being an internationally recognized playwright and author, Hischak has taught at both the high school and college level and is a retired professor of theatre from the State University of New York College at Cortland. A Fulbright scholar, Hischak has also taught and directed in Greece, Lithuania, and Turkey.

Performance Application

Unlimited amateur rights at a single location are granted with the purchase of this book. For performances at contests or other locations, a royalty fee of **$10 per play per performance** is due.

We hereby request permission to perform the titles listed below from
Plays of the American Experience by Thomas Hischak.

Scene(s) being performed: _____

_____

_____

Number of performances: _____ Dates of production: _____

Name of producing group: _____

Contact name: _____

Address: _____

_____

_____

Phone: _____

Email: _____

Amount due: _____

Payment: ☐ Check Enclosed ☐ Credit Card ☐ School Purchase Order # _____

Card number: _____

Expiration date: _____ Verification code: _____

Mail this application with your payment to:

 **MERIWETHER PUBLISHING**
A division of Pioneer Drama Service, Inc.
PO Box 4267
Englewood, CO 80155-4267
or
Email to: payments@pioneerdrama.com